Athar / SHLOMO KALO

Original Hebrew title: *ATTAR*

English translation by **Philip Simpson**

© All Rights Reserved
Y   D.A.T. Publications
POBox 27019, Jaffa 61270, Israel
Phone: +972-3-5071239
Email: dat@y-dat.co.il
www.y-dat.co.il
ISBN: 978-965-7028-60-5
3rd English edition November 2015
Printed by Amazon CreateSpace

Cover: age 4
Graphic design: Benci Sharon

Shlomo Kalo

ATHAR

Table of Contents

Preface

Few creative works are focused on solid facts, their active protagonists bearing real names, unfabricated nicknames, and at the same time diffusing a bold spirit of uncompromising authenticity, always astonishing, alarmingly plausible.

Apparently – the story of a concentration camp, strange indeed, far from conventional, established in the closing stages of the Second World War in Bulgaria, in fact – an episode of downtrodden hope, from which nothing is to be learned, and there is no human being under the sun who does not live its lesson, consciously or not, willingly or unwillingly. A narrative, defying the canons of style, about hatred stronger than death, love fit to shake the foundations of the universe, and man, demanding his legitimate right to self-awareness, of which no one can deprive him.

Grapes

A cluster of grapes. Ripe. Amber. A slice of sunlight radiating delusion. Inflaming expectation. Pardoning cynicism.

A left hand clutches a stalk. Bony. Skeletal. Sturdy grip.

Body, consciousness, soul: tense readiness to protect the amber treasure from any trespasser, lawbreaker, crazed with hunger.

A grape.

Plucked delicately, fingered gently, between finger and thumb, weighed cautiously, raised in solemnity blended with distant sorrow, put to the mouth, which waits with utterly commendable patience, laid on the plateau of a moist tongue... somewhere, in a corner of consciousness that is painfully lucid, arises the number "fifteen".

Repetition of the process. Another round: "seventeen"...

Half a kilo of this variety comprises between seventy-three and eighty-two units. No less, no more.

A cluster of grapes.

Left hand – steady.

Right hand – steadier still.

Left – clutching.

Right – plucking.

Grape after grape. Regular intervals of time. Identical. Metronomic.

Sun turning towards evening. Anaemic rays sliding over white walls, thick, ramshackle. Creeping inside.

Into the hiding-place.

A grape.

Gentle pressure between palate and tongue. Steadfast sweetness. Pure grape sugar, poetry.

Body, being, defiant biological unit, coming to life. With each and every grape. After each and every grape.

Body, being, biological unit, detached from everything that isn't defiant, coming to life, preservation of existence, demanding continuation, absence of belonging.

Dubious hiding-place. Breached from every side. Formerly – men's ablutions. A prisoner liable to appear. To attack. No rules in the camp. No law in the camp. No principles. A guard liable to surprise. To confiscate the bunch. In the name of the non-existent law. To lead the prisoner to the guard-house. For a flogging.

Body, being, biological unit, tensed.

Tranquillity in tension. Security. Expertise. Acquired over time. Product of the environment.

Tension. Even in sleep. In dreams too. Destroying what was, building what is obligatory. Without which there is no honourable survival.

Honour of the camp. Devoid of illusion, true to itself.

Honour of the camp.

The bunch will be finished. Spinning out the process yields no reward. Restraint is no solution. Distraction of the mind, no immunity.

Rhythm. Imperative. Dictated. Coercive.

Naked hunger.

Even for laws. Especially – for laws. For all the laws without exception.

Total hunger.

No human can stand it. No subhuman. No animal. A prisoner can stand it. Sub-animal.

One hundred and forty grams of bread per day. A dish of warm water, with six to eight kidney beans adrift at the bottom. No more. No less. Salt.

Work.

Transport and storage of inflammable materials. Transport and storage of toxic materials. Transport and storage of explosives and ammunition.

Heavy wooden boxes. Skeletons carry them. Into the gloom of the spacious warehouses.

Going back for more. Straight, left, inside, right. Box alongside box. Caution. To prevent disaster.

Water duties.

Three classes: Very Important Persons, familial, Gavroches, named after Victor Hugo's hero.

V.I.P.s don't go out to work. Familials - some of them. Familials do water duties. V.I.P.s don't do water duties. Gavroches do their jobs for them. In exchange for half a kilo of grapes. Every single V.I.P. has his preferred Gavroche. A V.I.P. chooses from among the swarming Gavroches, a preferred Gavroche. A V.I.P. pays a Gavroche for the duty. Half a kilo of grapes. A V.I.P. pays a guard fifty leva for half a kilo of grapes. The price of grapes outside - four leva for a kilo. The V.I.P. doesn't care. A V.I.P. buys himself half a kilo of bread for one hundred and forty leva. The cost of a kilo of bread outside - five leva. The V.I.P. doesn't care. He has money. Gavroche - just has Gavroche. Skeletal body. Rags. Standard clay dish and wooden spoon. Slice of moist bread, mixed with bran, about one hundred and forty grams. Daily ration.

Gavroche's privilege – to go out on water duty in place
of V.I.P. To be hitched to a barrel of water, instead of
a donkey or a mule or other beast of burden, to drag
a full barrel, four times a day, back and forth, up the
street outside the camp. He has the strength for this.
On hundred and forty grams of bread, plus salty, tepid
water, miraculously clear, plus six to eight white
kidney beans. He has the strength. To go out and do
his duty and the V.I.P.'s too. To earn, honourably,
half a kilo of grapes.

A V.I.P. is choosy.

Until a week ago he wasn't chosen. Not one out of
seven or eight V.I.P.s chose him. His appearance more
skeletal than the most skeletal of Gavroches. They
didn't choose him.

A week ago another V.I.P. arrived. A textile
importer. Has an official title too – "court supplier".

He chose him. Him of all people.

The new V.I.P. recognised him. Son of a regular
customer. He recognised the new V.I.P. too. He didn't
expect to be recognised, still less chosen. More skeletal
than any other. The youngest Gavroche of them all.
Dragging a barrel of water, an extra duty day in
addition to his own.

He was chosen. Extra duty. Dragging a full barrel
up the street outside the camp. Half a kilo of grapes.
A huge bunch, amber.

Sitting on the scarred tiles. Green and damp.
Plucking grape after grape. Slow rhythm, measured,
metronomic. Knowing with absolute, unequivocal
clarity, knowledge not to be denied from any
perspective whatsoever, in any manner whatsoever,
sober knowledge that there is an end. The bunch will
be finished. Stripped clean of all its grapes. All that is

left in his hand will be a greenish stalk, its naked thorns a depressing sight.

If he had believed, he would have prayed with every grape. A comprehensive prayer. Particularly long. A simple prayer of thanksgiving. If he had believed.

The day turns towards evening. In another half hour the cart will roll into the compound with supplies for the guards. He will stay close to the thick wall, jump inside. Steal a tomato or two. A cucumber or two. The carter doesn't see, doesn't hear. The carter pretends he doesn't see, doesn't hear.

About an hour from now – parade, distribution of bread.

The forbidding Asiatic plain.
Not the Hungarian pusta.
Not the American prairie.
Not the Russian steppe.
The forbidding Asiatic plain.
Attila.
Genghis Khan.
Tamerlane. The forbidding Asiatic plain.

Parade

Two lines.

Gavroches, geriatrics, familials, V.I.P.s

Orders.

At ease.

Attention.

At ease.

Attention.

Census.

Fall out.

Representatives of the huts receive the bread from the duty guard. Take it to the huts. Measuring with the help of a piece of ruler. Cutting with a thin steel wire. Equal slices. Distribution. Behind the back of a chance Gavroche, a laconic man in his forties, representative of the hut of the Gavroches and the elderly, lifts up slice after slice. The Gavroche calls the name of the recipient.

The bread is distributed.

Bread.

One hundred and forty grams. A thick slice.

The resolute vow, repeating itself, to no avail, every evening. Vow. To save the bread for tomorrow. To save some of the bread for tomorrow. Not to eat it now. Leave it till tomorrow.

His hand, forcibly clutching the slice, trembles.

Tomorrow - he'll wake up like a frantic beast. Beaten. A biological unit different from any other biological unit. Unknown. Not appearing in any catalogue. Not belonging to any order, super-class, class, sub-class, genus, strain. A biological entity standing in its own right. Unclassified. Existing.

Order - hunger, super-class - hunger, class - hunger, sub-class - hunger, genus -hunger, strain - hunger.

Living despair. Human. Prisoner. Sub-animal, Hunger.

The vow repeating itself, with the determination that can move mountains from their places. Same result.

Had he believed - he would have bent the knee, put hands together, vowed his vow, his gaze fixed on the Heavens.

There are no Heavens.

Ceiling. Thick. Plastered. Hostile. Censorious. It has not experienced hunger. It does not experience hunger. Isn't hungry. Isn't human. Isn't sub-animal. A ceiling.

In the hut - twenty-eight Gavroches, a laconic man in his forties, twenty-three geriatrics.

Geriatrics don't go out to work. They clean the camp, tend the gardens around the guards' quarters. Receiving the same bread ration, eating the same bread ration, the same kidney beans in tepid salty water.

One of them snuffed it last week. Didn't get up from his filthy cardboard bed on the rough wooden floor. If it had been possible to devour him, they would have devoured him. Twenty-eight Gavroches, ages between fifteen and twenty-five, a laconic man in his forties, twenty-three geriatrics. They would have swooped and devoured. Impossible. He was taken out of the camp. Swallowed up in the abstract infinitude of the outside.

Vanished.

Guards commanded Gavroches to take the corpse out. To dump it on a cart hitched to a horse.

Guards give orders, the job is done. Any job.

Guards order Gavroche to hit Gavroche. Gavroche hits Gavroche, with all the strength that he can muster, with all the severity of degradation. The one who has been hit, falls. The guard hits the hitter. With all the strength that he can muster, with all the severity of degradation. The hitter falls. The mouth of the hitter, who has collapsed at the feet of the guard, on the solid wooden floor, drips blood, his nose drips blood. His eyes are open. Blind.

Silence in the hut.

Guard goes out.

Just doing his job, carrying out his duty.

Respectable salary-earner, responsible member of society.

Let them see and let them fear.

The guard doesn't comprehend the reality into which he's been thrust. He doesn't need to. Carrying out his job, meeting his obligations. Let them see and let them fear.

No one sees. No one fears. He is like the Gavroche who is sprawled on the floor, unconscious, blood on his lips and his nose congealing. Eyes open, not seeing.

Sub-animal.

Not seeing, not fearing. No particulars. No generalities. No machinery. No systems. No biology. Sub-animal.

Hunger.

Piranhas.

Sub-animal. Sub-piranha. Sub-piranhitude.

Saint Gregory of Sinai was asked: "What is a man to do if Satan puts on the image of an angel of light and tries to mislead him."

He answered: "In such a case man needs superior powers of discernment in order to distinguish between evil and good."

The answer of an enlightened one: "It is impossible, absolutely impossible for Satan to put on the image of an angel of light, unless men have cast him so."

A sub-animal does not ask.

Does not answer.

Doesn't need saints.

Doesn't need any creature.

Doesn't despise any creature.

Pure being.

Sub-animal.

Cleansed of everything that is not he.

Free-born.

Cannot be diverted from his path.

Cannot be driven out of his mind.

Has no relations, no memories. Past, present and future.

No.

One objective. One destination. No existence, no non-existence. Clear thought, rapid, acute, pure thought. Non-thought.

Human.

Complete.

Not superior. Not inferior. Not sub-human.

Sub-animal.

Ask – and it shall be given you, seek – and you will find, knock – and it shall be opened to you. For everyone who asks receives, and he who seeks finds, and the one who knocks – it will be opened to him. (Matthew VII, 7-8)

Gavroches

Gavroches work. All the Gavroches without exception. Some of the familials evade work. Some, who are not skilled at evasion, work. Very important persons don't work.

All are obliged to work. All are subject to the penal system.

Very important persons pay an indemnity. Doesn't always hit the mark, doesn't always help. An indemnity, which is nothing short of a bribe. Annoys its recipient, puts pressure on the giver. Sometimes, not often, the camp-commandant, a police officer corrupt from foot to head, from head to foot, takes one of the very important persons out of the lines drawn up on parade, usually the evening parade, after which the bread is distributed, and strikes him with his whip, in full view of the silent ranks standing to attention and three poker-faced guards, until he collapses at his feet.

The indemnity-bribe doesn't help. An officer corrupt from foot to head, from head to foot, has his honour. Personal, exceptional, inscrutable, precluding definition. The honour of a police officer corrupt from foot to head, from head to foot.

All the Gavroches, all of them without exception, go out to work after the morning parade. On their bodies – relics of the clothes in which they were arrested, interrogated, sent to the camp. Their own clothes. The Bulgarian government is tight-fisted.

Prisoners have no right to clothing. Nor to food either.

The Jewish communities bear the cost of food. On an assumption of three daily meals per prisoner, and lavish provision.

The Jewish communities ask to bear the cost of clothing. On the basis of the same calculation. Request denied.

Bulgarian establishment.

Complies. Rejects. Deliberation – that is its right. Owes no explanations.

Bulgarian establishment.

Very important persons receive parcels every week. Not through the post. Every one of the very important persons has a personal courier. Loyal. Bringing in parcels, huge ones.

The guards carry the parcels to their own quarters. Open them. It's their duty. To check and inspect, inspect thoroughly and check carefully, lest there be any attempt to smuggle in something that is contrary to regulations.

The guards know well what is forbidden and what allowed. Most of them have four years of education behind them.

Very important persons receive only what they are allowed to receive: comb, soap, shirt, trousers, apron, underwear. Condensed milk, pastry cakes, sausages, cheese, smoked meat – are confiscated. The guards confiscate everything that is contrary to the law. That is forbidden by the law.

The personal couriers of very important persons come and go week by week. Until the personal justice mill of every V.I.P. is well oiled, the grinding is accelerated, and it will liberate him from the camp.

The personal justice mill of every single V.I.P. does not just grind the air. Every month, on average, a V.I.P. is freed, without another V.I.P. coming to take his place. Within not such a long period of time, the camp is liable to be completely emptied of V.I.P.s.

The personal courier of the V.I.P. has an inalienable right, to a personal conversation, of ten minutes duration, with his employer. From his personal courier the V.I.P. hears news of his family, of conditions outside, of new decrees, and of old decrees rescinded. The V.I.P. is a source of information worth much more than gold, to prisoner and to guard alike. An oracle, all of whose predictions come true, in every minutest detail.

A courier brings to his employer a number of banknotes, notes worth a thousand apiece. One of them is handed to the police officer, the camp-commandant, immediately after the personal conversation. Another is shared among senior N.C.O.s A sergeant-major rates five hundred. The monthly salary of a sergeant-major, is twelve hundred. A note for a thousand – and half the confiscated goods are returned to the addressee.

Most V.I.P.s grow fat in the camp.

The camp is infested with lice. V.I.P.s throw their underwear in the latrines. New, silk underwear. Every day. They're not used to lice. Clothes lice and head lice. No pubic lice. As well as lice – bugs. As well as bugs – fleas. The guards are clean of lice. Gavroches – swarming. Working hard every evening to dislodge them, better still – destroy them.

Uncountable numbers of lice. Infecting every square centimetre of the rags hanging on the skeletal body, concentrated in the stitching. Dense, extended columns, especially in the stitching of underwear. Clumsy lice. Impossible to count. No point in trying. Destroy them. Sometimes, a Gavroche succeeds in scrounging a burning cigarette-end. Passing the embers over the extended, ponderous lines, moving at a rate of a micron per hour. The lice explode, with variable sound, from the crackle of popcorn to machine-gun fire.

Very important persons throw silk underclothes on the tip. Gavroches know what they're worth. Try to estimate.

Very important persons, seven or eight in the entire camp. Seven or eight pairs of silk underwear... multiplied by thirty, multiplied by... the time thus far. No point going on. No one knows how long he's going to stay in the camp. No guessing, no approximation, no probability.

The guards calm them down. By order. Lest riots break out. They know all about the compulsory calming administered by the guards. All the same, they pay attention. Repulsive self-deception.

No point estimating. Does no good.

In the hut – a pickpocket Gavroche, seventeen years old. The rubber body of a circus acrobat. Wonderfully long fingers. A virtuoso pianist, a pianist of international repute, would envy him his fingers.

If it had been possible to steal time, the camp-pickpocket would have stolen it. Before it was too late.

The seventeen year old camp-pickpocket, with the fingers of a virtuoso pianist, the rubber body of a circus acrobat, would have put an end to grinding expectation, pointless, hopeless.

In the dim twilight, after the bread parade, the camp-pickpocket slips into the guards' well-maintained compound, finds a cigarette end that a guard has thrown away without extinguishing properly. Goes back to the hut, sits on the rough floor, pulls off the belted underwear, expertly passes the ember, revived by a light breath, over the columns of lice concentrated in the stitching. Perforated masculine underclothes. Their rags – the festoons of solemn weddings. Gavroches sans-culottes, makers of the French Revolution. Minions of Robespierre. His victims.

The resourceful camp-pickpocket, emits the strains of the machine-gun sonata in varying rhythm, to the approval of his attentive audience.

With the manners of a perfect gentleman, the camp-pickpocket offers the rest of the fag-end to the Gavroche sitting beside him.

Instead of machine-gun volleys, there is the pitiful crackling of popcorn, strident, inharmonious, irritating.

"Scarface", according to rumour a violent criminal, transferred to the camp from the prison, like a number of the Gavroches, like the laconic man in his forties, takes the cigarette butt from the inexpert hand of the destroyer of harmony, throws it on the floor and crushes it with what is left of his rough boot. No one dares say a word to "Scarface".

And you shall know the truth and the truth shall set you free. (John VIII, 32)

Scarface

An altercation between old man and Gavroche over sleeping space. Each claiming that his neighbour has violated the boundary. Hysterical voices. A sentry, standing a dozen metres from the hut's only window, hears them.

Scarface rises from his place, fells the old man with one blow of the fist, Gavroche – with two.

At that moment the camp sergeant-major enters the hut, accompanied by an extraordinary police officer: height – two and a half, breadth – two and a half. A walking fortress. Grey, watery eyes. Low forehead, roughly hewn. Thick eyebrows, uniting above an aquiline nose. Utter lack of expression. Vacancy of Buddha. Goliath, without the pride or the sense of humour. Frankenstein's monster – an angelic infant compared to him.

Sergeant-major points to Scarface. Two blows, sufficient to level the walls of Jericho, descend, one after the other, with sublime serenity, on the scarred face of Scarface. Scarface sinks to the floor, in a space vacated just in time by its occupants. The Buddha-style void withdraws about half a pace. Takes up his position behind the sergeant-major.

With his gleaming boots, the camp sergeant-major kicks the unconscious body, kicks and kicks again. In the belly, the chest, the back, the mouth, the forehead. Kicks and kicks again.

A clear stream of blood glistens between clenched lips, thickens, crawls over a broad scar, falls to the floor, spiralling. A narrow, tranquil rivulet, slow and constant. A cascade from the nostrils, joining what is already there, thickening, widening, urging. Eyes not open.

Sergeant-major goes out. On his right boot a few fresh stains, cherry-red. Still moving, changing shape. Scarface remains on the floor. Without moving. No one approaches him. No one says a word. The one whose space is taken by the inert body, takes Scarface's space.

No air.

Empty. Not the emptiness of Buddha.

Total emptiness. The asthmatic old man in the corner, isn't wheezing at all. For the first time since he was brought to the camp. Not a splutter, not even the preamble to a splutter. No longer will he treated to a juicy flood of curses and invective. No longer will he attract attention. No longer. He is cured. Cured of his asthma.

Morning light.

Parade.

Very important persons to the right, members of families, men and women, in the centre, Gavroches and geriatrics - left. As in all parliaments. As in the French Revolution.

Scarface they will clear away. Like that old man, who suddenly snuffed it. His body doesn't move or stir. One hour. Two hours. Three. All night. Not breathing. No one approaches him. Scarface - leprosy or plague. They beware of infection.

Morning light.

What is left of Scarface lies frozen on the floor. In the very same posture. Without the slightest movement. If he isn't dead yet, and doesn't show up on parade, he'll be dead before long. Unwritten laws of the consummate human being. Sub-animal. Devolution. Darwin laughed at God. Paid no attention to what members of his own species are capable of doing, he as much as they, maltreating one another without any help from God.

Sub-animal.

Laws. Not to be circumvented. Devolution - an established fact. Proof against denial. Pure science.

Shuffling into straight lines. Scarecrows. With the exception of very important persons and a few familials.

The broad back of the camp sergeant-major, greeting the parade.

A twisted face, a twisted smile, are not to the taste of the sergeant-major. A whip to the head. Command - to pick up the boulder by the gate, make a circuit of the camp, running, put it back in its place. A suitable task for a champion weight-lifter. The skeleton who has absorbed the blow of the whip smiles an ingratiating smile into the green eyes of the camp commandant, runs to the boulder, threads skeletal hands beneath it, takes, lifts, runs, tries to run. Tries to create the impression of running. A guard follows him, encouraging him to run with his whip. The skeleton runs. The whip behind him. Unforgettable sight. A miracle. The encouragement of the whip and its stimulation, an elixir, secret formula yet to be discovered by medical science.

Skeleton runs. Massive stone in his hands. His own body-weight. Skeleton rounds the wall of the camp. Guard runs behind him. A light, rhythmic, impressive run. The whip never stops issuing its vigorous encouragement.

Skeleton reaches the gate, carefully returns the boulder to its place. Calculation of pure mathematics. If the boulder is not laid in its original place, the skeleton will have to repeat his circuit.

Stretched lines. Very important persons, familials, Gavroches, geriatrics. Sergeant-major still showing his solid, inoffensive back, to his charges.

Bishop Diadorus, quoted by Saint Nikophorus, floruit 14th century: "He that is forever steadfast in his heart, is detached from all the attractions of this world, and taking the spiritual path, he will not be tempted by the desires of the flesh. This man will continue on his way, protected by his superior merits, serving him as his loyal bodyguard, until he reaches his pure objective. Then all the subtle and brazen wiles with which evil tries to confront him, will be doomed to failure from the outset."

Sergeant-major executes a solemn, measured "about-turn". In his right hand a whip, with which he taps lightly, lovingly, the palm of his left, thick-fingered hand.

Order, to bring out the corpse of Scarface.
Two of his neighbours on the floor from the hut of the Gavroches will drag the corpse to the tool store.
Four Gavroches will lift the corpse. Carry it, lay it on the bare wooden planks of the supply wagon. The head will loll this way and that, to the rhythm of the

trotting of the horse. The body will travel outside. By order.

Free. No longer hungry. No longer human. No longer sub-animal.

Free, like the cadaver of the old man.

Sergeant-major moves along the line.
Command.
Slow in coming.
Slow, still.

With heart devoid of vitality, ugly with curiosity, in the grip of pure, absolutely impersonal panic, Gavroches and geriatrics try to follow, without being exposed, the movements of the sergeant-major.
Middle of the line. Command.
Not yet given.
Angle of the eye, changing.
Sergeant-major.
Stops. Stands. Facing a wretched Gavroche. Command.
"Run with the stone!"
No.

A grey, indifferent morning is kind to Gavroche. The sergeant-major, before him, does not command him to run to the stone. This Gavroche has a guardian angel. Gavroche's nickname – Scarface. His face: puffed up dough, like hallah-bread. Colours: blue tending to black. Violet and purple. Eyes – two narrow, sharp slits. Breathing venomous, bubbling hatred. Pure. Absolute. Exclusive.
Sergeant-major.
Moves from his spot.
Continues along the line, pacing.
A measured pace, stiflingly slow.

Sergeant-major. Average height. Spherical head. Doesn't take in the transmissions sent by the slit eyes of Scarface.

Obtuse?

No.

He takes in, with pleasure. Paces with pure confidence. Complete, absolute, exclusive.

Scarface.

The triumph of devolution.

A saint who cannot be afflicted. No torment invented for the repair of his soul, no affliction devised for the advancement of his soul. A saint unpersecuted. Consummate. Sub-animal. Human.

The shadow of the ghost that was, that is not, that no man wants, that does not want itself.

Shadow of a ghost.

Living.

Saint Barzanophius and Saint John, living in the sixth century A.D., who subsisted on one loaf of bread per week, with nothing added, asserted that he who believes in God and clings to Him, will in the end be nourished by the Holy Spirit and have no further need of material food: "He is not hungry for material food and does not desire it. When he takes a morsel of bread, he will be as one who is utterly satisfied and does not covet it."

Scarface, After

Israel.

Marries a wife. Two sons. Employed by the water authority. Doesn't turn up for work. Sends in sick-notes. Harassed doctor confirms everything that Scarface demands he confirm. Harassed works manager covers for him. Day after day, week after week, month after month. A year.

Wife unfaithful.

Scarface informed.

The man involved is informed that Scarface knows, the wife is informed that Scarface knows. They do a runner. Scarface's father approaches his son, to mediate. Peace in the home. Two punches. The mediating father is sprawled in the street, unconscious. Needs medical treatment.

No more mediation.

Scarface visits his father in the hospital.

Reconciliation.

The man disappears. As if the earth has opened up and swallowed him. Some say he went to Australia. According to another account, he changed his name and emigrated to Brazil.

Another year.

The body of a young man is found at the bottom of a cliff-face, on the coast near Bat Yam. Skull smashed by blows from a heavy implement, large stone or iron bar. The corpse has no face. A black hole, empty. Identification impossible.

Scarface arrested.

Interrogated, released. Solid alibi.

A woman is brutally beaten by a man with a scarred face, at the busy central station, in the heart of Tel Aviv. A crowd of shocked onlookers. A succession of vicious blows. The woman collapses.

A police officer who happens to be passing prefers to look the other way. The woman – Scarface's wife. Needs hospital treatment.

Scarface disappears. The rumour: he has emigrated to the United States of America.

Grandpa brings up his children.

Scarface – the end.

Go and proclaim so that all Jerusalem may hear, saying thus says the Lord: I remember you, the kindness of your youth, the love of your betrothals, when you followed me in the wilderness in a land unsown. Israel was holy to the Lord, the first fruits of his harvest, all that devour her shall be denounced, evil shall come upon them, says the Lord. (Jeremiah II, 2-3)

Pitta

Work.

Gavroches and a number of familials.

Sun breaking through, clear air. Blue sky, deep and pure. Smiling.

Sensation: stomach.

He is nothing other than stomach.

Protesting, rebelling, irritating.

Stomach.

Hunger.

Obtuse. Cruel. World-embracing, devoid of pretension. Torturing and tormenting without pause, torturing and tormenting without respite. A fortress, impregnable, invincible.

Hunger.

The level of consciousness is scrupulously cleansed of thought, sensation, imagination, inspiration. Level of consciousness is bright, pure, whole, smooth as a mirror, stretching from infinity to infinity.

A brilliant idea mars the consummate smoothness of consciousness: to devour the stomach.

Yesterday, after the distribution of bread, the routine of vows.

Prodigious efforts to close eyes.

Eyes closed. Hand, a head resting on the arm attached to it, clutches spasmodically at slice of bread. No one could prise it from this grasp. Not even the skilful camp-pickpocket, the one with the pianist's fingers and the rubber body of an acrobat. The one who wants to filch the slice, will have to saw the hand off. Even when the eyes are closed, even when the entire biological unit is immersed in sleep, even when the entire biological unit gives up the ghost.

Eyes closed, hand closing on fresh bread ration. One hundred and forty grams! In the morning he will be empowered to take on the monster, force it to the ground, vanquish it finally, wipe it once and for all from the face of predatory reality.

Swoop on the slice, tear at it, tear again... No. No swooping, no tearing, tearing again, no and no. Pluck off, with angelic concentration, a crumb, and focus both eyes on it, gaze at it long and hard, penetrating the innermost depths of its essence, studying without let or hindrance, analysing its structure in the minutest detail, becoming acquainted with all the molecules of which the crumb is composed, learning to reel them off by heart, getting down to the atoms which constitute the molecules... bringing it with a measured movement to the parched lips, which are parted slowly, putting it into the void of the mouth on the tongue, as deep as is possible, so that not one molecule of it, of the crumb, will go to waste, flooding it with saliva, chewing it delicately, swallowing it calmly, confident in the knowledge that this isn't the last, and it will be followed immediately by another, and then a third, and then a fourth...

Ingenious plan.

The monster shall be defeated!

Sub-animal. Consummate human.

He is not stomach. They don't call him stomach. His name is – saint. Consummate human being. Whom none of the temptations of the world can overcome, who will not be led astray by anything. The truth will be revealed to eyes that long for it.

Salvation, faith.
   Sinking into sleep.
   Pleasant?
   Abhorrent?
   Sleep.
   Dreaming. A dream that is clear and bright, pure and free: climbing a high mountain, its summit – precious light. Mustering all his efforts, his being, his truth – to reach the summit.
   He will reach the summit.
   Climbing.
   Climbing.
   A steep slope becoming ever steeper. Smooth as glass. Using hands, clutching at every available hold. Panting, air growing thin. Climbing on and on, making no progress. Dragging his body. His skeleton. How lucky he is, having a body that's only a skeleton, so convenient! Feather-weight. Any heavier load he'd be unable to drag – way beyond his strength.

His skeletal fingers clutch at hollows. His fingers fasten on hollows, sinking into them.

The mountain puts on a friendly face. No longer smooth as glass. Someone has taken pity on him and softened it.

His skeletal fingers, stiff as talons, sink into hollows. These aren't hollows. Soft, amiable material constitutes this magic mountain. Bread! Whichever way he turns – bread! A high, steep mountain – bread! All of it bread!

Snatching, snatching some more, insatiable, snatching and gobbling, without respite...

Waking up. His mouth snatching and gulping the compressed air of the hut, the heavy stench, impervious, indifferent darkness, snores of the old

men from the corner.
Oppression.
His hand closes spasmodically on something.
Bread! To hell with vows!
Swoop, guzzle, rip apart!
Fingernails rip.
Hands rip.
Lips rip.
Teeth rip.
Tongue rips.
Saliva. Saliva by the gallon!
Hands, empty. Fingers clenched. Sleep
Go back to sleep.
No vows. No dreams. No bread.

Storehouse for explosives and ammunition. Sand floor. Heavy boxes. Wooden boxes. Carry them carefully. From outside – to inside. From inside – to further inside. Two skeletons to a box. Setting them down according to instructions coming from the lit doorway.

Man in army uniform. Giving instructions in a measured, miraculously clear voice, where to put a box, which box to take.

Distant doorway, lit up. Dazzling sunlight.

Distant.

More secure.

What is stored in the boxes is liable to explode. Fling into the air the skeletons handling it, shatter their limbs. Blow out the thick, shadowy walls of the cavernous warehouse, set it ablaze. Would the man in army uniform, issuing his instructions in a clear, even voice, survive the blast? Doubtful. Despite the cordon sanitaire. Very doubtful. He goes on issuing instructions. He knows. Still, he keeps his distance.

Going up to the camp. Lunchtime. Warm water. Salt. Six to eight kidney beans. Back to work. Waiting for the army man to arrive. Sitting in the giant shadow of an oak tree. Waiting for instructions.

On the bridge – peasants. Walkers, donkey-riders, wagon-drivers. Coming and going. Averting their gaze from the skeletons in rags. Not asking questions. Knowing.

A peasant stops. A canvas knapsack hangs on his shoulder, stuffed full to overflowing. He's making some sort of calculation, coming to a decision. A vigilant glance, this way and that. No guard in sight. He comes down to him, stands before him. Silently, puts a calloused hand into the knapsack, takes out a pitta. All white, ceremonial, virginal. A pitta! Will he offer it him? All the cells of his skeleton vibrate, charged with electricity. Incredible to relate – the calloused hand of the peasant silently proffers the holiest thing of all worlds, which has taken on the material shape of a pitta. He presents it to him.

He takes it.

Sub-animal. No longer. Weeps. Clutches end of pitta between finger and thumb. Firm grip, instinctive. Instinct of survival. Looking up and giving thanks. Gratitude that reflects all the goodness of God, his light, his mercy, his infinitude, his love, life eternal.

The peasant is embarrassed. He didn't expect such a reaction. He can't even manage a smile.

Before his bewildered eyes, the pitta is plucked from his grasp. Gavroche plucks it, with a bold, violent, irresistible movement. A fraction of a second. He goes away at once, taking his spoil with him.

Between finger and thumb, a tiny residue remains. Without a word, the peasant hurries back to the bridge. His eyes downcast.

The one who snatched the pitta devours it then and there. In a moment. A ravenous dog could not compete with him. Sub-animal.

Brings to his mouth the tiny gobbet that remains, held between finger and thumb. Doesn't let go of the morsel until it has penetrated deep into the void of his mouth, close to his gullet. The tongue moves cautiously, shifting the morsel. For a long second the morsel is suspended between palate and tongue, then pressed delicately to the palate. All the saliva glands emit thin streams, soaking the crumb from every side, calling into action all the administrative and mechanical cells of the skeleton, delving into every molecule of carbon. Consciousness celebrates, raising to its surface golden fields of wheat, stirring in the breeze, pure sunlight, endless drapery of sky, uniting together in every single molecule of the individual morsel, melting and disappearing between palate and tongue, approaching the gullet, sliding into the oesophagus, without arousing in it any digestive activity whatsoever.

Done, finished.

Situation reverts to normal. No golden wheat, no pure sunlight, no endless drapery of sky.

Stomach-man. Demanding. Insatiable. Eyes staring in all directions. Perhaps the peasant has distributed another pitta to another Gavroche like him. Perhaps, that Gavroche is the scion of a good home, is well-mannered, like him will not take the pitta from the peasant's hand without thanking him, looking up and uttering a polite, soft, sincere "thankyou", like him. He will swoop with the speed of lightning, grab the fresh pitta from his hand. The whole of the pitta, fresh, white, virginal, like a bride dressed up for her wedding day. One hundred to one hundred and fifty grams net, dough that has been kneaded and baked according to all the hallowed rules, in force since the day man was created and instructed to eat bread. Fine dough, not long out of the oven.

He will do this to that wretched Gavroche, from a good home, as to one who has done the same thing to him. Stole from his hand the gift that the peasant gave him, with that practised agility, learned in the concentration camp, that nothing can stand against. With his skills he will prevail over the one who robbed him. He will surely prevail! Any number of times, from every angle and every viewpoint.

The peasant has gone, departed in haste, swallowed up by the earth. He has distributed no more pittas. He will distribute no more pittas. The peasant is learning. No point in feeding a sub-animal, that doesn't know man, doesn't know God, doesn't know itself. Sub-animal. Sublime ignorance. Man. Escape from him. Keep away.

Reality.

Robbed, robbed. Rob, rob.

Would he do this?

He will die there and then – and not do it.

Sub-animal.

Flawed.

The army man arrives.

A whistle.

Paralyses every functioning brain cell.

Back to the boxes.

Pairs of trained skeletons. Lifting, in accordance with the instructions of the army man. Dragging, in accordance with the instructions of the army man. Disappearing into the darkness. Depositing, in accordance with the instructions of the army man. And back again.

Trudging along a broad dust road. On the highway, scraps of meat and potatoes. Someone spilled them, with malicious intent or in innocence, wickedly or inadvertently.

In a flash, the four straggling lines, striving, absurdly, to march in military style, become a strident, unruly rabble, swarming over the scraps of discarded food. Two guards on escort duty, brandish whips. With great energy. Raw flesh of prisoners, lean in the extreme, indifferent to whips.

Two minutes.

The road is stripped clean. Cleaner than it has ever been before. Ranks re-form and straggle on. Their splendour restored.

Ludicrous efforts at marching.

Between the jaws – morsels of fermenting potato, slivers of rotting meat. The digestive process set in motion, all cells fully engaged. Everything digested. Including the maggots and the worms therein. Everything. There's no subduing the stomach of a stomach-man. It will not be humbled.

Saint Simeon, of the tenth-eleventh century, says:

"It is hard for a man, who prays a long prayer over many things, to be aware of everything that his lips utter. But a man who prays a short prayer, with a few words, is aware of every word that leaves his lips. Those whose minds are not clear, need long prayers. The man who has learned to clear his mind, his short prayer is succinct and efficacious."

Punishment

No water. The sergeant-major, informed of the breaking of ranks on the way back from work, sets an armed guard on the barrels.

No water. Not for washing, not for laundry, not for cleaning the hut, not for drinking.

Throats are parched.

Washing, laundry, cleaning, don't obsess the mind. From any perspective whatsoever. Total cessation of washing, laundry, cleaning. Pre-emptive cessation, before it's demanded.

Drinking.

Throats are seared.

Minds go up in flames. Eyes stare. Imagination creates mirages of foaming cataracts. Niagara. Adding oil to the fire.

Through the window of the hut, beyond the fence of the camp, some fifty paces, under the guard-tower, clearly visible – a tap of burnished brass. Massive tap. They fill the barrels from it.

Tap of burnished brass. Massive tap. Open day and night. Water streaming, day and night. Full of power and noise. A flood of limpid water, fit to quench any thirst. Even an elephant's thirst. A dozen elephants. A herd of elephants.

Tap. Without a key to close it. Its rhythmic flow used to soothe the slumber of Gavroches and geriatrics. Till today. Till this evening. This evening – it's driving Gavroches and geriatrics out of their minds. Throats parched, convulsed. Bodies parched, convulsed. Eyes – frantic.

Thirst. Thirst can be endured. Outside the camp. Not after a day of gruelling work. Not as a supplement to murderous hunger. No human skeleton can endure thirst. No sub-animal.

Fingers clenched, stretching. Clenched, stretching. No one lies in his regular space. No one sits in his regular space. They are all standing. Geriatric and Gavroche. Silent, tense, taut. Listening to the running water. Its cheerful, uncaring rhythm.

Water.

Laconic in-his-forties has a suggestion. Laconic in-his-forties, transferred to the camp from prison, like several of the Gavroches, has an idea. Laconic in-his-forties, serving a ten year stretch for robbery, corruption, intimidation of witnesses, threats. Transferred to the camp with two-thirds of his sentence still to run.

Idea.

They listen.

To approach the sentry, ask him to fill a jug with water from the abundant tap, in exchange for a suitable sum of money...

What sum? – he is asked urgently, in the rasping, venomous whisper of deranged humanity.

Laconic in-his-forties decides: everyone will pay two leva, for two gulps of water.

Everyone has two leva to spare.

Except him.

Two leva.

A respectable total of one hundred and four leva. In exchange for two litres of water. More perhaps.

Collection proceeds, in silence.

One hundred and two leva, not one hundred and

four.

He doesn't have two leva.

Sent away, confined to the corner.

Utter darkness.

Who will approach the sentry? Laconic in-his-forties.

Takes the jug. Capacity two litres, more perhaps. Takes the money. Waits

Patience of a highwayman.

Waiting.

Till the sentry, pacing rhythmically, turns towards him. Notices his silhouette, takes his hint. Like a customer in a café, waiting for the waiter to notice him and approach him.

Time. Darkness. Tension growing heavier. Every nerve stretched like a bow-string. Unbearable.

They bear it.

A fateful moment. If the hint, for some reason or other, is not to the liking of the sentry and he ignores it – the last hope is lost. Laconic in-his-forties will pay the price.

Hint.

Of a man of experience.

Cannot be ignored. Impossible not to respond to it. Beyond the ability of the human soul, not to respond to the hint of an experienced man. It's the nature of the soul, its essence.

Hint.

Pure resolve, irresistible. The hypnotic assurance of an experienced man.

The sentry approaches.

Laconic in-his-forties holds out an empty jug, held in his right hand, with confidence, of source obscure. One hundred and two leva in his left.

Without a word, the sentry takes the empty jug in his left hand, one hundred and two leva in his right. Walks away.

He walks down the slope, the same route followed by the duty barrel-haulers and those taking the place of the duty barrel-haulers in exchange for half a kilo of grapes.

For a moment the bubbling flow of water is halted. Stopped by the filling hole of the clay jug. The jug has a hole for filling and a nipple for drinking, located in the curved handle. Clay jug.

Long moment. The cheerful thrumming of the water resumes. The sentry walks steadily up the slope, the same slope that drains the energy of the barrel-haulers, those on duty and those taking on the duty in exchange for half a kilo of grapes.

Rhythmic squeaking of new boots.

Laconic in-his-forties holds out two skeletal hands, protruding from the broad sleeves of a tattered, threadbare tuxedo.

Sentry holds out a full jug. Laconic in-his-forties takes it, skeletal hands shaking for a moment. Watchers in the dark hold their breath.

Full jug of water, safely within the jurisdiction of the hut. Sentry turns away. Laconic in-his-forties, in a metallic whisper, gives the command to form up in extended line. The line curls around, along the dark walls of the hut. Dense. Tightly packed. The chest of one pressing into the back of another. Eyes scurrying about in the gloom. Glowing like hot embers, predatory.

Water.

Laconic in-his-forties. Lifts the jug ceremoniously, puts his lips to the nipple. Gulps. Two full gulps, clearly heard by all.

Hands it to Scarface, who stands at the head of the line. Scarface follows his example. Two gulps. Big, refreshing, noisy – and no more. A matter of honour. Or – correct assessment of the situation. Jug. Passed on to the next.

Laconic in-his-forties accompanies it. Hearing the sound of water trickling down arid throats, attentive to the gulping. Counting: one, two.

Laconic in-his-forties is quick to snatch the jug from the quivering lips of geriatrics who have forgotten how to count up to two.

His mind is running amok. Imagination: throwing himself into fire, jumping from a ship into the sea, shooting himself in the temple with a heavy revolver, just so long as he won't have to hear any more the sounds of an outrageously hateful world, or see its sights, just so long as he won't have to hear any more the gurgle of water in parched throats, so there will be an end to his torment.

He doesn't know himself.

Heavy, dense darkness.

A tall old man passes the jug to the old man next in line, much shorter than he.

His hands get there before the hands of the aged homunculus, clutching feverishly at the jug, lips glued to the nipple. No power in the world could detach his lips from the nipple of the jug.

Blows land on his head, his nape, his face, kicks on his buttocks. Witches' hands tear at his hair, mouths bite his flesh.

His firm stance is not impaired, not to the slightest degree.

Indifferent to the pain. Any pain whatever. A full,

refreshing gulp, and another. And no more.

His hands and his lips relax. A vicious fist draws blood from his nose. Whisper: when he has it, he'll pay! A parting kick.

Laconic in-his-forties imposes order.

The straggling line forms up again, in the Stygian gloom.

Water.

Body, air, water, food. Lethal dependence.

Globe of the earth. Jail.

Habitual criminals.

Air, water, food.

Body.

Saint Gregory of Sinai, *floruit* 14th Century, declares: "Departure from corruption is taken by some to mean progress on the spiritual path, while others define it as total detachment from the sensual."

And he goes on to say: "Thoughts are the language of the Devil, and the vanguard of lust."

Washing the Dishes

Attracting attention.
Compassion?
Solidarity?
Affection?
A peasant handed him a pitta, in preference to all of the other twenty-seven Gavroches. In the detention-centre in the capital, on his way to the camp, a pickpocket was commanded by a sharp-eyed inmate to give him back what he had pilfered from him. In the solitary-confinement cell of the regional prison, to which he had been committed for lack of space in the local detention-centre, he was presented with a cup of tea – hot and sweet and invigorating – on behalf of a group of convicts who witnessed his unceremonious arrival. On the train journey to the camp, the escorting officer was asked, by passengers who had made his acquaintance, to allow him a share of their bread, cheese and fruit.
Bread parade.
Lengthy twilight.
Low skies. Copper clouds.
A middle-aged guard calls him. To wash the guards' dishes. Fifteen dishes of glazed ceramic. In exchange for leftovers of meat, properly trimmed, spiced. Nectar of the gods.
Every mouthful crams the cells of his skeleton with sparkling light, molten, flowing, alive.
Sufficiency

The systems of his body – celebrating.

Festivities ending.

Ended.

A distant sense, strangest of all, of satisfaction. Partial.

To work. Fifteen dishes of glazed ceramic, like the dishes used by the prisoners. Greasy. Unlike the dishes used by the prisoners. His own dish is washed quickly, in water from the barrel. Sometimes – it's hardly worth washing. The tepid, salty water, without any vestige of grease, makes the job easier.

To wash dishes.

At home a housemaid did this job. A lively rustic, smiling, young, giving satisfaction.

New law: No Christian to be employed by a Jew.

In the place of the rustic, a middle-aged Jewess, gloomy, slow-moving, giving no satisfaction.

His mother did not wash dishes.

In his childhood he had once or twice watched the impressive process: soap bubbles on plates, pans, cutlery.

A guard brings a can of water. If it's not enough – fill it from the tank inside.

He's left in the darkness, on a patch of sand, behind the guards' quarters.

Water. It won't shift grease. The guard forgot the soap. A diffident knock at the door. Asks to see the guard. The guard, face blank. No affection, no cooperation, no consideration. Obtuseness.

Has he forgotten the soap?

Astonishment.

There is no soap.

Just water?

Sand.

Where?

Plenty of it out there. Got hot water, haven't you?

He returns the way he came. No soap. Fifteen dishes stacked on the patch of sand.

Scrapes with sand, rinses with water. The grease stays.

Scraping again, rinsing again. The grease stays.

Tries the reverse. Soak with water, pour water away. Sand, scrub, rinse. No effect.

You can bet peasants know how to shift grease from dishes using sand and hot water. Beggars too.

To be born peasant or beggar – what a blessed state that would be!

Look at him. Studying, exams, books. Proud parents, envious relatives.

He doesn't have the faintest idea how to clean dishes with sand and hot water. Or even with soap and hot water. Any means whatsoever. Not the shadow of a ghost of an idea.

His eyes are moist. Stress. Creeping, impervious, dominating all else, obliterating all else. Impossible to resist. Choking.

Stress. All this time – through arrest, interrogation, torture – he hasn't shed a single tear. He hasn't known stress of this special, abysmal kind. He's going to forfeit this prime "assignment".

Every Gavroche knows how to wash dishes. With whatever material comes to hand. Hot water and sand.

Every Gavroche – except him. Why did they choose him? High forehead, fine facial lines, unvanquished by affliction, sincere look. Exceptional, even for an adult. His face isn't the face of a Gavroche. In any sense, from any angle. Skeletal though it may be.

Different.

For better or for worse.

Different.

This time – for worse.

Why is that simple people – peasants, travellers, prison guards – are so misled as to find his appearance attractive, the cast of his features exceptional, empty of content though it is? What would he not give, not to be himself, not to have been born as he was born, in the family into which he was born. To change his appearance, change his talents. Once and for all.

To know how to wash dishes.

With sand and hot water.

Hunched over every dish individually. Drop of hot water, handful of sand, vigorous scrubbing, more hot water, rinse. All there is to it. Fifteen dishes, made of glazed ceramic. As identical as fifteen drops of water. He stacks them up. Two towers.

Takes them inside.

Void lit up by electric bulb. The guards' quarters. Generator supplies electricity.

A guard sits on the bench, reading an old newspaper. Without looking up from the paper, silent, he points to a broad shelf of white, unvarnished wood. Dishes are to go on the shelf. He dismantles the towers, arranges the dishes neatly, trying hard not to make a noise. Says goodnight. The guard doesn't answer.

Goes out.

The night is young. The stars – living jewels.

Hope.

The hut of the Gavroches.

The camp pickpocket approaches him.

He's been waiting for him. Bad news with a smidgeon of good. The guard was disappointed. The job wasn't done properly. Obviously, he had no idea how to do it. A more capable Gavroche is needed.

This he heard, eavesdropping under the open window of the guards' quarters.

If caught, he'd have invented some excuse. Hunting for cigarette-ends, maybe. He'd be let off with a slap in the face.

The young man's gleaming eyes are fixed on his. Mischief, entreaty, demand.

If he goes back to the guards' hut and recommends him, the choice will be that much easier for them. His chances of acceptance – realistic. In exchange – he'll hand over to him the water-duty of his V.I.P. That way, he'll have two stipendiary duties to do. His V.I.P. can be trusted, as can his own. A request, from a friend to a friend, between brothers in destiny – to return to the guards, recommend him.

Again he retraces his steps.

A hesitant knock on the door.

A guttural, rasping, incoherent voice.

Goes inside.

Hostile looks. He turns to the guard who called on him in the first place, apologises for his lack of skill in washing dishes. He knows a young man who is well qualified to do this work. Arrogant indifference is replaced by keen interest. The camp pickpocket will be the chosen one! Distant pain of loss. He passes on the name, wishes them goodnight. Leaves.

High skies, of regal velvet. Stars. He can breathe easy. The appointment has been transferred. The camp pickpocket will cheat him, hand over his V.I.P.'s duty to someone else, make an extra profit on the deal.

That's to be expected, required by the logic of the camp. An exchange here, an exchange there. There are no rules in the camp, written or unwritten. No canons of behaviour in the camp. Lawlessness - is the law.

The soul is at ease.

Without any vows this time, he cuts the bread, puts it to his mouth, digests it crumb by crumb. Tonight he'll sleep soundly, peacefully. Replete and consoled. No more dreams about mountains of bread, no more dreams, no more.

The camp pickpocket, seventeen years of age, is summoned to wash the guards' dishes. Performance satisfactory.

Surprisingly, he keeps his word, transfers his V.I.P. to him.

A month passes.

In exchange for a pack of "Thomasian" cigarettes, the camp pickpocket hands over his new assignment to a hunch-backed Gavroche, nineteen years of age, who is in the habit of describing over and over again, in precisely the same words, to anyone prepared to listen or simply to himself, the feast that his parents laid on for his bar-mitzvah ceremony, recalling one by one and in the minutest detail all the delicacies served on that occasion. The pack of cigarettes is traded by the camp pickpocket with a desperate smoker, a family man, for a loaf of bread.

The sharp-lined face of the camp pickpocket, smiling. Always, and at all times. Twenty-four hours in a day. A mischievous, cunning smile. Even in sleep. Appealing sometimes, sometimes - annoying, always encouraging.

For I desire goodness, and not sacrifice; and the knowledge of God more than burnt offerings (Hosea VI, 6).

Before

Almost thirteen years old. School. On the whitewashed walls, photographs of prime ministers, senior officials, dead patriots.

Disciplined class.

Bulgaria.

The teacher: "Our brave friends, our invincible allies, will be passing this afternoon through the streets of our capital. Go out to the squares, the streets and the highways, wave flags and handkerchiefs to greet them, smile your friendliest smiles! Give them autograph books to sign. Our brave friends, our traditional allies, who will never be defeated, have conquered half the world, and now they are on their way to conquer the rest. They are with us, as we are with them!" – An emotional, patriotic tirade from a middle-aged teacher, her thin, Clark Gable style moustache bristling with every impassioned word emerging from her lips.

They go out to the streets, the unpaved roads and the squares.

Children.

A passing army detachment. Armoured vehicles, trucks, motorcycles. Handkerchiefs waving. Here and there – a pennant with a swastika symbol.

Children

A motorcyclist stops alongside a group of handkerchief-wavers, pushes up on his helmet a pair of steel-framed goggles, the type worn by welders.

Urchins from the junior classes of the school

gather around the fantastic figure.

A heavy raincoat, grey, made of rubber. Grey helmet. Look of a victor dispensing favours. Grey.

Urchins from the junior classes produce little notebooks. The superman, the hero who has conquered half the world, and is on his way to conquering the rest, smiles, signs willingly, confidently.

A girl of about nine years old, in a flowery frock, holds out a tiny notebook. Her friend catches the eye of the star of the show, points to the one proffering the book and declares in a clear voice: *"Jude!"*

The smiling motorcyclist, the invincible conqueror of the world, figure from legend, isn't smiling now. With an authoritative sweep of the hand, just the one, he sends the proffered notebook flying through the air.

The new notebook lands in the mud. Its gleaming white pages are soiled.

The girl turns away.

Laughter.

The girl runs after her book, stoops, picks it up, tries to wipe the mud from it.

The girl weeps. Eight or nine years old.

All the sinews of his body are tensed. His lips quiver. Lips and legs are not obeying him. A pain that the void of the whole world could not contain. A yell. A frantic impulse to attack the grey, heartless monster, waging war against a skinny girl in a flowery frock, who hasn't yet turned nine years old.

Decision.

To do everything to fight the monster. Not a matter of revenge. To fight all-out war, unflinching.

The insult to the girl – is an insult to the whole world.

A feverish search, for organisations that have gone underground. Contacts – are avoiding contact. "*Hashomer Hatzair*" – has disintegrated. "*Hechalutz*" – no longer exists. "*Betar*[*]" – will fight on the soil of the homeland, not here.

What is left?

The devotees of Karl Marx, Lenin, Stalin. Fighting without compromise. All-out war.

He makes contact. Passes a short test.

A member of the Red underground. A codename. Takes on assignments, fulfils them. Eagerly. Writing manifestos and distributing them. Collecting contributions for families whose breadwinners are in jail. Food and support. Spreading rumours designed to undermine confidence in the power of the monster. Initiating new members into the subtle methods of the underground movement.

One sturdy young man, and another one, and he.

The dusk before dawn.

Fortified building.

Swastika flag fluttering on the roof. Tall, iron gate. A sentry-box on the far side. A soldier, in grey, marches back and forth. Nine and a half paces this way, nine and a half paces that way. A clockwork toy. On his shoulder – an automatic weapon. They press into the dense shadow at the corner of the building. At their feet – an empty canvas sack. Silence.

Each one of the three has a task. Defined, practised, learned by heart. The toy goes on pacing. Comes close to their corner, and turns away from

---

[*] Zionist organizations

them, to go back... with every intention of going back. The tough young man, the smiler, responsible for the deed, draws a black revolver, aims at the grey back of the toy. Squeezes the trigger. Still smiling broadly.

A deafening report. The toy stops. A thousand years of uncertainty, of hearts that have stopped beating.

The toy collapses to the ground.

Bull's-eye. The first assistant of the perpetrator takes the pistol from him and leaves the scene at once. The two others run to the toy, with the canvas sack. Remove the automatic weapon from his powerful shoulder, stow it in the canvas sack, and go, each his separate way.

From the tall building behind, shouts are heard, the racket of men in steel-shod boots pounding along wooden walkways, back and forth, crazed, panic-stricken.

He runs. With the heavy canvas sack. At the corner of the street, hands the sack with its contents to a man who asks him if the correct time is five in the morning.

Continues on his way, his body shaking. From head to foot. A liberating shudder. He is fighting against the grey monster, who spurned the autograph book of a little girl not yet nine years old. A skinny girl, in a flowery frock.

He knows people. Energetic, strong-minded, motivated. Not the kind to stand by and watch from the sidelines, or to sit on the fence. Those not so blind they cannot see, nor so deaf they cannot hear, who have declared all-out war on the grey monster, war without compromise.

I have said
You are God
And all of you children of the Most High
(Psalm LXXXII, 6).

Miko Papo

Lads in their bloom. Hopes. Dreams.

Objective: to eliminate a collaborator. His compatriot. Stout of build, tall of stature.

His compatriot, collaborator.

Five in the morning.

Miko Papo rings the bell of the thick door of the collaborator's apartment. No spy-hole. The door opens, a fraction. The collaborator, in pyjamas, half-asleep. Without hesitation, without waiting to be invited in, Miko Papo draws an automatic pistol, shoots his stoutly built compatriot, the collaborator, with seven lead bullets, from throat to groin. A full clip.

The victim staggers, collapses.

Not dead.

Gives a detailed description of the perpetrator. Of Miko Papo, who doesn't stand looking on from the sidelines, doesn't sit on the fence, is fighting the grey monster, war without compromise, all-out war.

The hunt for Miko Papo. The underground struggles to find him a refuge.

The plan – to send him to the hills, to join the partisans. They're waiting for their contact-man. He's late. They're still waiting. Tension. Patience.

There's no bed where Miko Papo can lay his head. There's no apartment that can accommodate him for more than one evening, if that. He gets money. Dyes his hair. Hides out in cinemas, a different one every day, sitting through two full showings, till midnight, grabbing a few hours of sleep if he can.

The hair-dye fades. Under the red, black is beginning to show, the curly hair of a youth who has just turned eighteen. Black curls appearing, formerly the pride of Miko Papo, the entertainer, the man of piquant sense of humour, who can stir up a tidal wave of laughter and admiration. Not looking on from the sidelines, not wanting to look on from the sidelines, not capable of looking on from the sidelines. A dauntless fighter.

Arrested, leaving a cinema.

A black night.

Interrogated. Tortured. Betrays no one.

Condemned to death.

There was no one to hold out a hand to him in his time of need, no one to find him a refuge. The underground could do nothing, was ashamed of its impotence. Miko Papo was led out to his death.

Eighteen years old at the time of his murder. He left no wife, he left no child. He did not leave Miko Papo. A final, impassioned cry, reverberating around the walls of the prison, "I'm going to die!" All the prisoners, from the apprentice pickpocket to the hardened murderer, from the visionary to the moron, respond to him. The thick walls quiver to the racket of the clogs beating against them, to the terrible cry of defiance, bursting from a thousand mouths:

"I'm going to die!"

The thick walls are helpless.

Miko Papo did not leave Miko Papo

Miko Papo did not leave ego.

Miko Papo.

Cast away from you all the sins wherein you have sinned and make yourselves new heart and new spirit, and why should you die, House of Israel? For I take no pleasure in the death of he who dies. (Ezekiel XVIII, 31-32)

Marko

Marko, younger brother of Jacob, the husband of Rivka, his cousin. A pupil at the technical school.

Marko. His instructor in "Hashomer Hatzair", six years his senior. Charismatic. Went up to the hills. A partisan.

Jews. Bulgaria. Expulsion from the capital city to outlying villages.

A question for the underground – how to act?

Answer: Go wherever you're sent, resume contact at a more propitious time.

With his mother and sister on a smoky train, climbing the flank of a steep hill.

A township, under the tall peaks of Pirin and Rhodope. That's where Marko is.

Coded correspondence with underground contacts. Week after week. Month after month. The time is ripe. To come forward. Matters have been arranged,

He removes the yellow Star of David from his shirt.

Goes to the contact.

He's to go back to the place he came from. The liaison man will find him. There's a password. He's authorised to organise a cell. He's given a pistol, a 6.35. Easy to hide.

He goes back. Organises a cell.

Gosho. Seventeen years old. Not Jewish. Son of a publican. Two Jewish boys, aged fifteen and seventeen. The day is approaching.

Gosho tells his father. His father acts.

The provincial governor is his friend. He lays the facts before him: a certain Jew has arrived in the capital, without a travel permit. He's removed the yellow Star of David from his clothing. The provincial governor summons the chairman of the local Jewish community, the highly esteemed Mister Selanikyo. Demands that he reveal the identity of the youth.

The highly esteemed Mister Selanikyo returns to the provincial governor. The name and address of the young man, recorded on a crumpled scrap of paper torn from an oilskin notebook. Lays it on the governor's desk, without a word.

A police officer comes to his house. He's arrested. His mother and sister are distraught. Not he. His thoughts are racing back and forth, like ants whose nest has been wrecked. Who betrayed? How much has been betrayed?

Gosho's father is no fool. He knows that outright betrayal, in the event of the regime changing, will cost him dearly.

He realises that the investigators are groping in the dark.

By agreement with the contact, the story they are told, over and over again: the boy missed his home town, and the girl he was parted from. That's all. He's harmless, really. The Bulgarian police are anxious to establish the truth of the story.

A prisoner, charged with the theft of a rubber tube, is heard singing, in the prison, a well-known, melancholy Schlager, about Sofia, the city of lights and allurements, and about a girl he met there, who broke his heart for ever.

Police officers don't distinguish between voices.

Not their job. Not their field of expertise.
Police officers hear a song. It fits. Smiles all round.
Sighs of relief.
The puzzle, according to the authoritative judgment of the police force, has been fully solved.
The investigator is told: "Jew-boy fancied a bit of skirt!"
Relieved laughter.
File closed.
Decision: Somovit concentration camp.

You have infused your spirit in mine,
As pure water is mingled with wine,
Whatever touches you – touches me,
For I am you eternally.
(al-Husayn Ibn Mansur al-Hallaj, Tenth Century)

Shlomo Kalo Reveals:

At fifteen years old I was arrested in my homeland, under the terms of a law which removed all civil rights from the Chosen People.

For a week I was held in a crowded cell at the local police station, and every morning, at precisely the same time and usually in identical circumstances, my body was treated to a regular and quite respectable quota of whip-lashes.

The flogger was a thin and tall man, meticulously dressed, serious, solemn – or perhaps "stern" would suit him better – who from time to time showed signs of weariness with the onerous task entrusted to him, but he stuck to his assignment and did a thoroughly professional job. With commendable precision, he administered exactly the right number of strokes to the soles of my bare feet. On account of my reasonable behaviour, his stocky and bull-necked assistant was relieved of his role in the process, which consisted of sitting, with his full weight, on the head of the one being flogged. This ploy was intended to prevent excess movement on the part of the floggee, liable to spoil the accuracy of the whipping, which might even miss the bare feet altogether – most unfortunate. A miss obliges the flogger to go back and start the process again, both because the inappropriate behaviour of the floggee must be punished, and because the effect of the series of blows up to that point has been impaired. In such cases the wrath of the flogger was liable to boil over and then he would revert to an effective albeit prosaic method – beating with both hands simultaneously.

To be fair to the floggers, they certainly earned their crust from the table of authority. They fulfilled their role without exception, without exaggeration and without shirking. Only a few of them would attain a kind of ecstatic release – relishing the job for its own sake – and with their wholesale ruination of the quotas, and their snorting, like wild boars in rut, blasting the ears of their victims, and the ears of their assistants and their own ears with all kinds of juicy oaths, and their final arrival in a trance-like state, not an uncommon phenomenon – at this point they needed replacement by a less impressionable flogger, and a good dowsing with buckets of icy water, to cool the purple, sweating and tearful head.

In that provincial detention-centre, the inmates were stubborn, cunning and irascible and at the same time – avoiding contact with those more irascible than themselves. Their motto – "Do to others before it's done to you!" – was deeply engraved in their rancorous hearts, and they held true to it in every sense and in all circumstances.

One of them was subjected to what was considered a highly prestigious form of chastisement, this being twice the normal number of strokes, applied with vigour and enthusiasm by two floggers, replaced as required. He was accused of stealing a rubber hose two metres in length from the local railway station, a charge which the man vehemently denied. He was flogged ten successive days without respite, twice and sometimes thrice a day, and all the time he maintained his claim of innocence and didn't vary his story by so much as an iota. On the tenth day, in the absence of proof or of a confession, he was released. He came to take his leave of us, the other prisoners, and with a cunning smile on his unshaved and deathly white face, revealed:

"The hose – I've still got it!" and he disappeared.

They sent me to an improvised concentration camp at the other end of my homeland in flesh. I was transported from one detention-centre to the next by regular passenger train, accompanied by a guard who was replaced at every station. Every one of the guards who escorted me turned to me solemnly with the same offer, expressed in precisely the same words: "Behave yourself – or its handcuffs?"

I always opted to "behave", so I was spared that particular inconvenience in the processes of eating and defecating. According to the laws of that country, prisoners are not supplied with food – even if it means starving to death. But I didn't lack for food. Passengers on the same train, aware of the law and its implications, were happy to share their food with me, and with the agreement of the escorting officer, who always received a generous portion himself, I took whatever they had to offer.

At one of the intermediate station, I was thrown into a cell which, to my surprise, was almost empty, and for this reason looked spacious. On one of its bunks, infested with lice, bugs and fleas, sat a balding man of about forty years old, his lanky body confined by heavy chains, attached to two iron balls – each weighing some ten kilos. The man's gaze was serene and relaxed, like one who has completed the task allotted him, and has done it properly, to his complete satisfaction.

He didn't say a word, not even responding to my hesitant, somewhat awkward greeting. As became known to me later, he used to be the owner of a butcher's shop in a small township in the hills, and when he caught his wife in the arms of her lover, he took his cleaver to them, beheading them both and proceeding to dissect her body with professional precision – ribcage here, offal over there, legs, arms etc. – just as he used to treat cattle carcases.

We both passed a sleepless night. Neither of us uttered a single word. The long, densely packed, dull-red columns of bugs, and the straggling, hyper-active ranks of lice, crawling over us from all directions, in provocative fashion, with insolent, untrammelled indifference, formed an almost physical bond between us. The fleas for their part jumped and cavorted with a kind of isolationist gloom from every corner, and surprised us all – the former butcher, who twitched slightly whenever a flea landed on his leg, me, with my rueful smile, and the serried ranks of bugs and lice, moving in military formation, and then retreating and scattering in confusion, hurriedly returning to their former dispositions and their tight phalanxes, on the departure of the prancing flea.

The next detention-centre into which I was thrown, the evening of the following day, was totally different from its predecessor – crammed with human bodies, sweating one another's sweat, defecating where they stood, and inhaling without protest the pungent stench that filled every space. This was one of the detention-centres in the capital city.

About an hour after my arrival, a man was brought

in whose mind was seriously deranged. He was claiming, adamantly, that the queen of that country, whose husband, the king, had been murdered a few days before, had invited him to marry her. A declaration of this kind constituted, so it seemed, an infringement of the law. The pretender to the throne was arrested, interrogated, and refused absolutely to renounce his claim. No way was found to convince him of the gravity of this refusal and its potentially dire consequences.

The man was pushed forcibly by the guards into the tightly packed mass of bodies, where at least he faced no risk of falling. So he stood there, immobile, and still standing, fell sound asleep, emitting from time to time a grating snore.

The snoring was not an agreeable sound to those prisoners forced to stand close to him, and being unable to get away from him, they decided to play a joke at his expense. They woke him up, with considerable difficulty and informed him, with all due solemnity, that while he was asleep, envoys had arrived from the palace, to take him to the king's widow.

The man immediately began knocking on the armoured door of the cell, something never to be done except in a case of sudden death or an outbreak of fire.

In response to his urgent knocking, a juicy curse was heard from outside. For a moment the man hesitated, then, still driven by his insanity, knocked on the door again and again with redoubled vigour, with clenched fists, to the accompaniment of knowing, scornful smiles all around.

A long moment of silence passed, suffused with tension, boding no good. And then, suddenly, the bolts shifted in their casing with a cold, authoritative sound, metallic, intimidating.

The door swung open and a blast of cold, blessed air penetrated the dark void, crammed with bodies.

The man took a step forward, with dignity, with an absurd, childish air of self-importance. The guard raised his rifle, and slammed the steel-rimmed butt into his forehead with all the strength he could muster.

The man stopped, tottered where he stood and fell back, among the prisoners, the expressions on their faces still knowing and scornful. His forehead streamed blood and he was losing consciousness. The door was closed again with a thunderous crash, and we were left as before – packed tightly together, scores of bodies, in the embrace of the heavy, fetid stench.

A long time elapsed before the stricken man regained his senses. No one recognised him. He wasn't the same as the man who had been thrust among us just a little while before, the tone of his voice confident and his stance erect. This was not the same person at all. His back was stooped, his face contorted, and the manic gleam had been wiped from his eyes. These were the eyes of a normal person, meaning – the eyes of a hunted animal, desperately seeking a refuge that does not exist, cowed into abject submission.

His forehead, scored by welts of congealed blood, was turning blue, and swelling. He was unrecognisable, a changed man indeed. And when somebody mentioned the business of the king's widow, he couldn't understand what was being said, and he was looking round trying to identify the maniac who had been nurturing such absurd delusions.

I asked myself then: does this man not owe gratitude to those prisoners, who in the malice of their hearts devised that tasteless prank, that so-called "joke", and to that guard who dealt him a blow that was all crude, unrestrained violence, and yet in spite of this, someone took the trouble to turn him into the unquestioned envoy of pure compassion and grace of the kind that is hidden from mortal eyes? Anyway, that dream, the fata morgana that deranged his mind – is it not the product of a certain culture, the culture of this wretched planet on which we are standing, if blatant insanity can indeed be called "culture"?

And we according to his promise look for new heaven and new earth, where righteousness dwells.
(Second Epistle of Peter, III, 13)

Marko, After

There was no chance of going up to the hills, to meet the charismatic Marko, brother of the husband of his cousin, Rivka.

The meeting would take place, as they used to say in the underground, "after victory!"

Victory! The venomous monster had been humbled, had breathed its last. No longer would monsters in grey uniforms and with grey minds insult and injure little girls.

Decisive victory. Absolute.

He was in no doubt at all he would meet Marko and the two of them would tell one another of their activities in the dark days. Calmly, and with an eye to the future as well. It wasn't going to be easy, ridding him of all that had accumulated during those dark days. He was sure of this, beyond any doubt.

Marko's brother, when asked, had a story to tell:

One of the partisans in the platoon was wounded. Marko was chosen to take him to a woodcutter's hut in the forest. The woodcutter was to be persuaded, by means of some unequivocal threats, to go down to the nearby township and fetch a doctor. Marko had a comrade there to help him. They came to a broad woodland clearing. In the middle of it – the hut where the lonely old woodcutter lived.

The comrade was told by Marko to climb to the top of a tree and watch out for any developments. To warn of danger with a bird-call. The order was obeyed. Armed with a Schmeiser, a pistol, two grenades filled with buckshot, Marko knocked on the door of the woodcutter's hut. The door was opened. The wounded man was carried inside, laid on the bed.

The threats proved effective.

The woodcutter saddles up his donkey, takes his axe, sets off down the narrow path leading to the township in the valley nearby. He disappears from view. An hour later, the hut is surrounded by members of an elite anti-partisan unit. The look-out in the tree is taken by surprise. He wonders, in his own words, which is the preferred option – to warn Marko and thus endanger all three of them – the wounded man, Marko and himself, or stay where he is and wait to see what transpires. He decides to keep out of sight.

A loudhailer tells Marko that he is surrounded on every side. His immediate, unconditional surrender is demanded. He slings the wounded man over his shoulder, tries to shoot his way out through the cordon with the pistol. A hail of bullets drives him back to the hut.

The wounded man is mortally wounded now, and he dies. Marko storms out again, throwing his two buckshot grenades, firing the Schmeiser, crying out in a clear and passionate voice that is heard far and wide, reverberating in the ears of the troopers and of the watcher hidden at the top of the tree: "Long live freedom, death to fascism!" His last words.

A man shall live
And not see death
He shall save his soul from the clutches of the grave,
Selah (Psalm LXXXIX, 49).

9. 9. 1944

Servants of the monster are retreating.
Going underground. Changing identities.
Servants of the monster are retreating.
Slipping away and disappearing as if they never were.
New government. Seeking consolidation. Chasing after the monster's servants who are running for their lives. Uncovering their hiding-places. Intending to bring them to justice. Proclamation: it will bring to justice all those who have forgotten the meaning of justice.
Monster's servants in retreat.
Members of the provisional government chasing after them with commendable revolutionary fervour, without respite, without mercy. Monster's servants are well aware of how far it can reach – this "justice" of those who until a few days ago were being hunted by them. Monster's servants, running for their lives, are still as dangerous as ever.

A police station only recently vacated by the monster's servants. Reports.
One of the monster's servants has found refuge in the local library. Trying to change identity.
The mission: to arrest him and bring him to the police station, which is now in the hands of the revolutionaries and has a new name – "People's Militia Headquarters". All the old names, the pre-revolutionary names, have been changed. Before long,

there will not be a single street or installation that has not been renamed.

To arrest the monster's servant, who has found refuge in the local library. The monster's servant is armed. Who will volunteer to arrest the armed monster's servant?

Silence.

Thunderous silence. Embarrassing.

Victory has been won. They are eager to start enjoying its fruits, living in freedom and peace. Without monster's servants. Victory has been won. There's no appetite for taking risks, not now, at the very last moment. Caution is what is needed.

Who will volunteer?

He will. Ashamed of the others. Ashamed of himself.

They give him a pistol: a Walther 7.65. Nice model. Aerodynamic design. Walther 7.65, with a full magazine.

Final briefing: remember, the man is armed! Disarm him first, arrest him, bring him back to Headquarters. He'll get a fair hearing. Due process of law.

Pistol in the pocket of his overcoat, hand in his pocket. Sets out on his way. In the former police station, they go on handing out assignments.

The street is empty. Once it was humming with people and traffic. Empty now. These are twilight times. No law and no judge. Better to hide away at home, behind locks and bolts. Peep through the window. Retreat from the window if someone peeps back at you.

Dangerous to walk the streets. Twilight times. Handy for settling scores.

Sit quietly in a locked house, behind closed windows, sealed curtains. Sit and tremble. What else is there to do - but tremble?

Local library.
Low, elongated building.
He goes inside.
In the middle - a table, on both sides of it - children. Eighteen to twenty children on either side. A long table. This is the beggars' quarter. Slum housing. Parents send their children to study in the library. The library is heated, homes are not. A warm library is a better place to study than the overcrowded one-room, unheated apartment that you share with nine others.

His entry arouses interest. The children put down their books, look up at him. They look scared.

At the head of the table, a man aged about twenty-five. Hair black, smooth. Hard face. He doesn't look up from the book, which he isn't reading.

The quarry.

He walks behind the row of children, approaches him. Draws the automatic. Walther 7.65, nice model, highly polished. Command:

Get up!

The twenty-five year old man, black hair, hard face, looks up from the book that he isn't reading. Rises slowly to his feet. A gigantic figure, eyes cold and contemptuous. Heavy hand raised in a sweeping, disdainful gesture, nearly knocking the pistol out of his hand.

Steps back just in time. Command:

Hands up!

This man used to be in the service of the monster.

He hunted revolutionaries, he tortured, shot, murdered.

He ignores the command.

The room in which he stands, the children sitting paralysed in their chairs, melt away and disappear.

It's just the two of them, he and the monster's servant.

He has no sense of how or when, but he is sure of one thing. His finger is squeezing the trigger of the automatic, aimed at the stomach of the monster's servant.

Squeezes the trigger.

The Walther responds – with a soft, fateful "click", blasting his ears like an electrical charge. Disaster. His heart freezes. All hearing is gone.

The monster's servant stares back at him grimly, his right hand, that showed his contempt for the aimed pistol, the one aiming it and those who sent him – moving towards his back pocket.

Not even aware of what he's doing, he pulls back the cocking mechanism. The dud is ejected. Time. His finger is about to squeeze the trigger again, on a fresh bullet. Not a dud.

The monster's servant shouts: "No!"

His hands are raised. Two massive hands of a tall and powerfully built man, a man of experience.

"No!"

He recovers his wits. Commands the monster's servant to turn round. Pulls a pistol from his back pocket. A Walther. Just like the one he's holding. Tucks it into the left-hand pocket of his overcoat.

They leave the local library, the children looking on in silence. The giant walks with hands raised, like a character from an American gangster movie or an English crime novel. Escorting him with a pistol cocked and aimed. This isn't an American movie or an English novel.

Heart serene. Eyes fixed.

On the way to the People's Militia Headquarters, the few people they meet freeze where they stand – or run for their lives. Curtains twitch.

Scores of pairs of eyes watch the child escorting, with loaded pistol, the giant who used to serve the monster, his hands raised, a picture of obsequious submission.

People's Militia Headquarters. The prisoner is handed over to the duty officer. Details recorded.

The prisoner's massive hands are cuffed.

He feels a strong impulse to hug him. To fall at his feet and thank him. For raising his hands in time. For shouting that paralysing "No!" A thousandth of a second before the confident squeezing of the trigger, driving the firing-pin against another bullet, a valid, lethal one. Before an act of violence, of murder.

Tears well in his eyes. Tears of gratitude.

To the One who stopped the first bullet and ordered the monster to raise his hands before the second shot.

Tears of gratitude. Gratitude that will stay with him as long as he lives on this earth.

His commanding officer, a severe man in his forties, a veteran of the International Brigades in Spain, reads the report. His comment: You put those children in danger.

What was he supposed to do?

His commanding officer, severe man in his forties,

veteran of the International Brigades, gives the matter some thought. Time passes. More time passes. Finally he declares:

You had no choice.

He had no choice.

Timur, Timurlenk, Tamerlane in European languages, born 1336 in Kesh near Samarkand, died 19.2.1405 in Otrar, near Chimkent.

One of his legs was shorter than the other.

The keen-eyed Persians noticed this, dubbed him "Timurlenk" meaning "Timur the Cripple". Timurlenk grew to manhood, conquered peoples, nations, lands, tongues, principalities. Persia, with all of its keen-eyed and sharp-tongued populace, was subjected to his sway.

Timurlenk shows his appreciation of the wit of his sandaks, their wisdom and equable temperament, by constructing majestic buildings on their land. Awesome buildings, the like of which no eye has seen, of which no ear has heard. From time immemorial, and forever.

Timurlenk builds pyramids.

Not in the Egyptian style. Not replicas of the Aztec step-pyramids.

Tamerlane's pyramids. Modest by Egyptian standards, and differing from all other pyramids, anywhere in the world, in terms of the construction materials employed.

No mortar, no pitch, no dressed stone, no brickwork, no adhesives. The technique of construction is a secret yet to be deciphered.

No mystery about the fabric of the buildings, which is simple, natural, familiar, requiring no manufacture, and cheap. The cheapest material there has ever been, or ever will be: human skulls. The severed heads of hundreds of thousands of Persians, men and women, young and old. Millions.
Pyramids.
Soaring to the heights. Masterpieces of technology. Visible from afar, and creating a stench that permeates every corner of the massive Persian principality. Birds of the air peck at carcases. Beasts of the land prey on carcases. Worms and maggots nibble carcases. They cannot compete with Tamerlane. With pyramids in the style of Tamerlane.

Timurlenk.
Timur the Cripple.
Tamerlane.

The forbidding Asiatic plain.
Not the Hungarian pusta
Not the American prairie.
Not the Russian steppe.
The forbidding Asiatic plain.
Tamerlane.

Bakish

The new, the extra V.I.P.
Tall of stature. Appearance: heavyweight boxer.
Expression: astonishment. Prolonged, unflagging.
Astonishment.
A prisoner, not coming to terms with his imprisonment. Doesn't understand. Refuses to understand. A reality, that isn't his reality. Refuses to accept. Refuses to challenge. Refuses to settle down. Reality, that isn't his reality, that doesn't exist for him.

Bakish.
Born: Sofia, Bulgaria. Parents emigrate to England. Unsuccessful foray into the textile trade. Childhood - London suburbs. Takes a job with "Dunlop". Outstanding employee. Studies production techniques, makes improvements. Sent, at his own specific request, to Malaya, major supplier of rubber resin, the one raw material urgently required by a voracious and affluent western society.
Dunlop tyres, Malaya.
Dose of malaria. He isn't beaten. The disease is.
London.
Bulgaria.
Suburbs of Sofia. Workshop. One ramshackle hut. Rubber products. Expanding business, taking on staff. Tyres, of all types, for all vehicles: bicycles, motorbikes, cars. Superior quality. Reasonable prices.
A factory. The sole tyre manufacturer in the Balkan

Peninsula. Flood of orders.

More personnel, more machinery.

Personal supervision. Of quality, prices.

Flood of orders.

"Bakish" tyres – widely reputed.

Bakish – manufacturer of reliable tyres.

Income in foreign currency.

The Bulgarian government is short of foreign currency. Needs foreign currency. Is thirsty for foreign currency, always has been and always will be.

Bakish supplies it. With a generous hand. In abundance. Like a burgeoning spring.

The Bulgarian government guards Bakish like the apple of its eye. A sentry on his door-step, twenty-four hours a day.

1933. The Nazi Kalpakchiev intercepts his car. Bakish's driver killed. Not Bakish. Kalpakchiev imprisoned. Murdered by Jewish convict.

The Bulgarian government doesn't understand how Bakish is managing to sell his products. Can't fathom out the open secret of a logical process. The Bulgarian government is incapable of fathoming out the open secret of a logical process. That's its nature. Every people, nation, nationality, tongue – has a nature of its own.

Bakish brings in a constant flow of foreign currency for the Bulgarian government. Arouses suspicion in the heart of the Bulgarian government. Is he on the level? He's checked out, checked out again. Questioned again and again. Watched like a hawk – is he going to do a runner, taking his fortune with him?

1935. Ford offers to bear the cost of paving all the major roads of Bulgaria, in return for an undertaking to import Ford vehicles exclusively. The Bulgarian government faces a dilemma. Decision: Ford is trying to colonise Bulgaria. Offer rejected. Major roads of Bulgaria will remain dust-tracks.

Bakish. Horn of plenty to the Bulgarian government. Brought to a sudden halt. His factories boycotted. Production collapses. No quality, no buyers. Bakish in a concentration camp, with criminals, Gavroches, family men, V.I.P.s.

No more foreign currency for the Bulgarian government.

Bakish.

Question: what does he do or what did he do outside?

Answer: high school student.

Has he heard of Schopenhauer?

He has.

Of the objective, which once attained opens the way to aspiration towards a new objective? The notion that satisfaction does not exist, it's an illusion?

He has heard.

Question: what if the objective is absence of objective?

Answer: absence of objective will never be attained.

How so?

Absence of objective is self-delusion.

For whom?

The one of whom self-delusion is demanded.

Of what kind of person is self-delusion demanded?

He who falls prey to self-pity.

He's rewarded with a hunk of fresh cheese on a thin slice of bread.

Bakish:

The concentration camp that's being built on the bank of the Danube has a specific objective.

Which is?

Transfer to a German camp, in Poland.

Is that good news or bad news?

They're killing people with gas.

What for?

Extermination of the Jews.

Where's he got that from?

From a reliable source. The fact is – they're bringing criminals in here, ones with long sentences still to serve.

What's to be done?

Pray for an end to all this.

Bakish, afterwards.

Israel, without a cent in his pocket.

Manufactures sophisticated rubber stoppers for water-bottles: Jewish construction workers for the use of.

Bakish. Israel.

Attempt at adaptation: rubber stoppers for water-bottles.

Meagre proceeds.

Competitor: plastic stoppers, not at all sophisticated. A third of the price.

Bakish.

Manufacturer of Bakish tyres.

Formerly.

One of the wealthiest tycoons of the Balkan Peninsula.

Formerly.

One of the respected personalities of the Balkan

Peninsula.
Formerly.
Bakish. Israel.
Childless.
Lives in what used to be a stable.
Hangs himself from the smoke-blackened beam of a former stable.
The end.
Bakish.

The forbidding Asiatic plain.
Not the Hungarian pusta.
Not the American prairie.
Not the Russian steppe.
The forbidding Asiatic plain.

Name: Attila.
Nickname: *Flagellum Dei* – "Scourge of God". Date of birth unknown, died 453 A.D., on his wedding night. Those who buried him and his treasure murdered, according to the terms of his will, by his relatives. Place of his burial unknown. Burial place of his treasure unknown.

Short of stature, elongated head, piercing eyes. Ruthless. Murdered his brother, Bleda, became king of the Huns. Sole ruler of half the known world.

Huns.
Horsemen.
Never dismounting from their horses, day or night.
Sleeping on horseback.

Eating, on horseback, the fresh, raw meat of their defeated enemies.

Raping the wives of their enemies.

On horseback.

No grass will grow beneath the hooves of their horses.

No animal will live.

No man arise.

Flagellum Dei. Scourge of God.

Vegetable, inanimate, animal. All expire.

The forbidding Asiatic plain.

Not the Hungarian pusta.

Not the American prairie.

Not the Russian steppe.

Attila. Scourge of God.

Even he must expire.

Cruel Evening

Hitch in the bread supply.
No bread.
Bread parade, without bread.
Cruel evening.
Everyone huddled in his space.
Silent.
A wounded animal, refusing to lick its wounds.
Let it bleed, let it be over.
Let there be an end.
No bread.

Laconic in-his-forties shatters the silence. Tells a story. From his past. A story. The Thousand and One Nights – the embodiment of solid, unassailable logic, based on attested and documented historical events – compared with his story.

Laconic in-his-forties, his story. A searing insult to any senile old man.

No one is smiling. Deep silence. Rapt attention. The words flow. No need to exercise discernment, judgment, logic. Everything thrown wide open. Soaring, above and beyond the excesses of the most unruly imagination possible.

The stomach is back in its place. Stomach-man sits in the darkness, not saying a word, mustering all his attention, listening to the words, describing situations, landscapes, eminent people of whom the narrator was a regular house-guest, welcomed always and at all times.

The story continues.

Associations dissolve every burden, break down every barrier, shatter every obstacle.

A mighty, overwhelming river of sheer illogic. The fire that ignited the brain cells is extinguished. The stomach under control.

Laconic in-his-forties, sentenced to a ten year stretch. Actions that society denounces as serious crimes.

Laconic in-his-forties.

A genius.

Accomplished cheat, robber, thief, suborner of witnesses.

A genius.

Relief. Ease. Relaxation.

The astonishing story of laconic in-his-forties.

Alarm.

Ten minutes to midnight.

Parade.

Bread.

Euphoria.

Grabbing.

Laughing.

Slapping one another's skeletal shoulder. Giving thanks. Invoking God.

Sleeping a deep sleep, the sleep of the just, dreamless sleep.

A Girl and a Boy

A girl and a boy were in love
Till the day they came of age
And it was time to be sanctified
To be married one to the other
In a ceremony of blessing, in the way of their fathers
In the ancient church.
The girl fell down on her bed,
The boy knelt at her feet:
"Ask, beloved of my heart, whatever you wish
I shall bring with all speed to your bosom, ask, do not
delay!"
"A bunch of amber grapes,
 My king, my love,
A bunch of amber grapes
Will raise me from my bed,
To arrive in time
For our wedding ceremony, as arranged
In our holy church!"
Winter across the face of the land
Grapes – who can find?
The boy leapt up on his horse
Made haste to Istanbul, the capital city
To do the bidding of his princess,
His soul with her soul bound,
In holy, never withering love.
The boy spurred on, without a pause,
Three days, three nights.
He came to Istanbul at the noon of the day.
In a rage he turned over market stalls,
Ransacked the shops and the storehouses,

Broke into dark cellars.
Found what the queen of his heart had requested:
Amber grapes.
For every grape, a golden shekel.
Again he mounted his horse, steely horse.
Three days he raced on, three nights,
Never once dismounting from his horse.
At noon-day he arrived
At the gates of his home town
Where his love awaited him.
At the door of the ancient church.
A priest chanting a psalm,
A burial service going forward.
The boy leapt down from his horse.
Knelt at the edge of the pit.
"Raise up the coffin!" he cried,
"Open it before me! Let me look upon
The pure, pale face of my princess,
Let me touch her cold hands,
That once gave me such angelic caress.
Let me lay a cluster of grapes on her breast,
And my heart at her feet,
While it is beating still!"

(Bulgarian folksong from the mid-eighteenth century,
based on a real incident.)

Gigantic Bug

New guard. Replacing the "walking fortress", who has been transferred to the central prison where, so it seems, they are crying out for a man of his exceptional talents.

Tall and solid, full-bodied. Thick neck, arched and rigid, leading the way to an angular head. A gigantic, clumsy bug. Big teeth. Rusty voice. Loud, hollow laugh.

He doesn't feel at home in the camp. Not among his fellow guards, not on the parade-ground, not in the hamlet, huddled on the torrid plain.

Thirsty for activity. Seeking diversion, and finding it.

Goes into the Gavroche-geriatric hut, starts kicking skeletons in a good-natured sort of way, with a gurgling laugh, wrestling with them. Friendly wrestling. Gavroches are too feeble to resist. To say nothing of the geriatrics, in line for every misdirected kick on offer.

New guard. Gigantic bug. Hollow laugh. Likes to play.

The camp pickpocket is offended in every cell of his lithe body. Kicks, blows. The camp pickpocket is inventive, has keen initiative. After the departure of gigantic bug he declares, with rancour, this has gone far enough, he has no intention of continuing to serve as punch-bag for any creature in the world, and least of all, for the low life-form that they call a guard.

The camp pickpocket sneaks into the precinct of

the guards' quarters, finds an empty matchbox in a garbage bin, fills it with lice. A multitude of lice. Goes in search of gigantic bug. Wrestles with gigantic bug, empties the box, to the very last louse, under the collar of the shirt of playful gigantic bug. Manages to get away in time, evades the playful iron fist.

Next day. Going out to work, returning. Bread parade.

Tense expectation.

No sign of gigantic bug.

Sent away on leave. Three days.

Three days of respite.

They pass.

Gigantic bug appears in the doorway of the hut. His massive body fills the frame of the door.

A rusty, forced, instructive laugh, a declaration.

He's got rid of the lice.

His wife insists these are Jewish lice. Nonsense. Lice are neither Jewish nor Bulgarian. Lice! He can't stand them. He would really like to play, but he's not taking any risks. His wife worked three whole days and nights removing the lice from his uniform. They crawl into every hole, every stitch. Especially, in the underwear. A constant itch, demanding to be scratched. Very sorry. Both sides played a fair game! Superb! Meaning: they, the Gavroches, on one side, and he, the guard – on the other. To his regret, and he is sure, to theirs as well, this enjoyable pastime must come to an end!

The camp pickpocket remains defiant. He confronts gigantic bug: That isn't fair! – A clear statement, declaration of emphatic dissatisfaction with the performance of a despised menial – Every evening they have waited for him to come, waited with longing, and now – utter disappointment! Bor-ing! Maybe – in spite of everything?..

Gigantic bug retreats in confusion from the onslaught of pigmy pickpocket.

He understands how he feels – he declares – but this is the situation! They won't be meeting again in the hut.

And outside? – asks young pickpocket, not giving up that easily.

We'll wait and see. In an official capacity – declares gigantic bug – no more wrestling! In conclusion, he sees fit to add with firm emphasis – Under any circumstances whatsoever! Anyone challenging him – will forfeit bread ration, water ration, kidney beans...

The threat works. Young pickpocket retreats to the shadows. Gigantic bug vacates the frame of the door. Fresh air floods inside

Young pickpocket follows gigantic bug out of the hut, watching him go with a look of smug satisfaction, the mischievous spirit of youth, amused to the very roots of his soul, then returning to the hut and intoning, with a lordly and imperious gesture: Begone! Avaunt!

At that single and unique moment, a mighty howl of laughter bursts from fifty-two frantic throats. All are laughing: Gavroches, geriatrics, laconic in-his-forties, even Scarface is laughing – an explosion of mirth, loud, resonant, and free.

And God created man in his image, in the image of God he created him (Genesis I, 27).

Pickpocket, After

By virtue of his status as a former concentration camp inmate, the camp pickpocket enjoys the trust of the new government.

Militiaman, sergeant, sergeant-major, officer.

Junior lieutenant, eager, finding ingenious solutions to complex problems.

Brilliant future.

Empties the safe at the local militia headquarters.

On the razzle for three days and three nights.

Caught.

Handcuffs.

Ten years imprisonment with hard labour.

The camp pickpocket. The end.

Declaration.

Behaviour.

Logic – declaration. Pogrom – behaviour.

Happiness – declaration. Senselessness – behaviour.

Concession – declaration. Brain cells dying – behaviour.

Radical reform – declaration. Mediation – behaviour.

Justice – declaration. Sealing the tomb – behaviour.

Truth – declaration. Lowing of calves – behaviour.

Freedom – declaration. Impotence – behaviour.
Loyalty – declaration. Stagecraft – behaviour.
Love – declaration. Scorched earth – behaviour.
Mankind – declaration. Sub-animal – behaviour.
God – declaration. Cain and Abel – behaviour.

David Four-eyes

Early morning of a rainy day. The heavy door of the hut is pushed open. A frightened, bespectacled creature stands for a fraction of a second in its frame.

A well-aimed kick in the hindquarters. A defeated creature, sprawled on the floor. In the centre. Hurried inspection of his spectacles.

New prisoner. Thick lenses. Tiny pupils darting around behind them. Innocence, submissiveness, capitulation, utter helplessness.

David Four-Eyes.

Thirty years old.

Bachelor. Former tax clerk. Not a Gavroche, not a geriatric, not a laconic in-his-forties, not a family man, not a V.I.P.

Early morning, misty.

David Four-Eyes. Cheap suit, made even cheaper by the tribulations of the road, to the furthest limits of the imagination, spread-eagled on the floor in the middle of the hut, checking his glasses thoroughly, inspecting his surroundings cautiously, like a cockroach about to be squashed, wary of the squasher who may surprise him, approaching from a direction not envisaged by his cockroach-senses.

Check and inspection. Glasses intact. Undamaged.

Slow rise to a crouch. Contraction of limbs.

Reality – a slap in the face.

There's no room for him.

He'll have to stand.

Eat standing up, sit standing up, grovel standing up, sleep standing up.

Bitter reality.

There's no way of contending with it, or obliterating it, nothing that can change it, or influence it. It can't be ignored, or forgotten. Reality. Fact.

David Four-Eyes is exiled to the threshold. On the threshold.

No one is prepared to give up a centimetre of his territorial space. Without exception. No Gavroche, no geriatric, no laconic in-his-forties. No one.

Through the ponderous dioptics, a defeated look. Crushed cockroach. Sub-cockroach.

Pure, absolute despair.

Pushed to the edge.

Surrounded by the tin pots used for nocturnal urination. If he lies there, they'll piss on his face, if he sits, they'll piss on his face, if he stands, they'll piss on his feet.

Reality, raw and naked.

No one gives a toss.

No one's prepared to give up a millimetre of his space. No Gavroche, no geriatric, no laconic in-his-forties. No one.

Naked reality.

David Four-Eyes.

Quite expendable. A narrow strip by the door, surrounded by piss-pots. A resting place for the ungainly body of David Four-Eyes. If he's incapable of standing, resting from work standing up, he can lie down with the piss-pots.

He tries.

They tread on him, curse him, kick him. Intentionally or unintentionally. Consciously or unconsciously.

Big tears mist the thick lenses of the glasses.

No one's to blame.

Let him complain.

Anguish, defiance, protest, revulsion.

Let him complain.

He complains.

Ten whiplashes. Bread ration forfeited. The glasses survive, miraculously. Curls up on the strip by the door. They piss on his face.

He doesn't utter a word.

You get used to anything.

Every morning, before parade, he's pulling lice out of his underwear. Standing by the wide, open window.

Extracting lice with meticulous care. Louse after louse. With the pedantry of a former tax clerk. Thoroughly.

For every louse dislodged, ten new ones come to replace it.

Continues delousing.

With care, without confidence, knowing it's hopeless.

Louse after louse. Nervous, not wanting to disturb anyone, spoil anyone's repose.

Extracting lice, with the dedication of a former tax-clerk. With curiosity. As if these are the first lice ever to be seen in the world.

A rustic matron is passing by on the narrow path on the hillside, overlooking the hut of the Gavroches and the geriatrics. Scandalised by what she sees: a bespectacled man standing at the window, underpants pulled down, fingers in his crotch. She approaches the sentry, indignant and affronted. The sentry turns to the sergeant-major.

She lodges a complaint, her voice quivering with emotion. A grievous insult. She's protesting on behalf of all women and their dignity, for the dignity of all humanity.

A couple of guards burst into the hut.

David Four-Eyes, still intent on the delousing operation. He's plucked from the window, dragged out like a sack of potatoes, on the way to the command-post. At the last moment, laconic in-his-forties succeeds in retrieving his glasses.

With the matron looking on, David Four-Eyes is kicked in the groin, over and over again, with heavy boots. More and more kicks, inflicted with impressive, intemperate vigour.

When the kickers tire of their work, their mates take over with whips and clubs, carrying on, under the sergeant-major's supervision, with vibrant energy, pure wrath, the task of lashing and pounding at the genitals of David Four-Eyes,

David Four-Eyes loses consciousness.

The matron weeps. Implores them to stop, call a halt, put an end to this. She withdraws her complaint. She's shouting, no longer caring about the affront to the human race, to all the women of the world. She curses the day she was born and first saw the light of the world. She falls on her knees, pleading.

Enthused by their work, engrossed in it utterly, like ravenous beasts, gorging on the entrails of ripped carcases, almost swooning in their euphoria, they pay no attention to the matron, her cries and her entreaties.

The matron rises from her fruitless kneeling, takes to her heels before her stomach turns over, while she still has her sanity intact. She disappears, the same way that she came.

David Four-Eyes is dragged back into the hut, dumped among Gavroches and geriatrics. Penis and testicles bruised and swollen to massive proportions, oozing blood.

One of the V.I.P.s is a doctor. Dr Rosenfeld. A physician of international repute. He is called, secretly, to attend to David Four-Eyes. Smuggled into the hut, he sees, inspects, diagnoses.

David Four-Eyes will be sterile for the rest of his life. It's incurable, irreversible. He can never sire children. Whether his penis will perform any of the normal functions of a penis is in doubt. Serious doubt, Dr Rosenfeld stresses. All the healthy faculties of body and of mind have been damaged by what the doctor calls "trauma". In the conditions prevailing in the camp – Dr Rosenfeld concludes – there is nothing that can be done.

Parade.
Only corpses are excused parade.
David Four-Eyes isn't a corpse.
David Four-Eyes is on parade. Present and correct. He must stand to attention like all the other prisoners. Keep his legs together, if he doesn't want another kick in the crotch.
They go out to work.
David Four-Eyes is looking for his glasses. Laconic in-his-forties has them. There's a price to pay for the glasses. Half a bread-ration. David Four-Eyes has no option but to pay. Laconic in-his-forties took a risk hiding them.
Gavroches agree with laconic in-his-forties. David

Four-Eyes gives up half his bread-ration, to the advantage of laconic in-his-forties. Gets his glasses back.

Work.

They cover for David Four-Eyes. Let him rest, in the shade.

Back to the camp. Gavroches reduce their narrow spaces, demanding, abrasively, that the geriatrics do the same. They do.

Laconic in-his-forties reduces his space.

Scarface reduces his.

There's space now for David Four-Eyes.

Under the window, where the air is fresh.

No more treading on his legs, no more kicking in the stomach, intentionally or inadvertently. No more pissing on his face.

Not any more, not ever.

David Four-Eyes smiles. An innocent, pure, distant smile, not of this world.

He's going to be sterile for life. Proper functioning of his penis in grave doubt.

He's accepted in the hut.

It was worth it.

Saint Simeon (Tenth-Eleventh Century), writes:

"The man who is privileged to discover that God, the giver of knowledge to humankind, dwells in his heart, who has studied the Holy Scriptures and plucked, like ripe fruit, the fullness of grace that the reading of them bestows – has no further need of books nor of the reading of them, knowing always who it was that inspired the writers of them... This man, who is himself a holy book, written by the finger of God, has attained all that is fitting to be attained, his task is accomplished."

Niso Makedonka

Niso Makedonka. Meets him in the V.I.P.s' hut. Evening.

In the V.I.P.s' hut, electricity. A bulb dangles from the high ceiling. The guards' generator provides power to the V.I.P.s' hut. V.I.P.s pay the full price. There are five of them left:

Bakish.

Dr. Rosenfeld.

Niso Makedonka.

Middle-aged man, profession obscure. Bags are packed. He's being released tomorrow.

Manager of an international bank. Lies on a thick mattress, reading a book. A sheet on the mattress. Fascinating book, evidently. Doesn't respond to his greeting.

Dr Rosenfeld, Bakish, Niso Makedonka, the one getting out tomorrow – they respond, each in his own way. Dr Rosenfeld – a cynical, dismissive reply, neutral expression. Bakish – contrived basso profundo, general air of gloom. The soon-to-be-released – limpid look, voice of a little girl who has just been awarded a merit star. Niso Makedonka – optimism hanging by a thread.

The hut. Same dimensions as any other hut. Like the hut of the Gavroches- geriatrics – where more than fifty men sleep on the bare wooden floor. V.I.P.s – there are five of them. From tomorrow – four. V.I.P.s have electric light at night. Gavroches-geriatrics – just have the night. Stygian darkness.

What is Justice?

Which is justice?

That which leads to repentance.

Justice of the V.I.P.s, to share with Gavroches-geriatrics: space, implements, foodstuffs. Justice of the Gavroches-geriatrics - to spurn the justice of the V.I.P.s.

Justice.

They are sitting in a distant corner, out of earshot, on chairs.

He's uneasy.

Sitting on a chair seems strange to him. The days he has spent in the camp have changed fundamental habits. Instead of chairs - floor. As if he had never sat on a chair before.

Sitting on a chair - betrayal of Gavroches-geriatrics.

He sits. Listens.

V.I.P. is agitated. Blue, clear look. Face of an elephant. Optimism, covering depths of torment.

He has to reveal certain things to him.

Three days from now, he'll be released. He has it from a reliable source. Freedom is on the way. He, Niso Makedonka, will be released three days from now.

Dramatic announcement. Hanging in the air. Left hanging in the air. It makes no impression on the youngest of the Gavroches. He makes no effort to pretend happiness, sorrow, amazement, envy. He's immune from all these things. Liberated. Stomach-man. Sub-animal. Complete human being.

V.I.P. continues. Prisoners will be transferred to shacks. Ten days from now. On the hill. New wooden buildings, comfortable. Sleeping on bunks, not bare floor any more. V.I.P.s will be released, to the last of them. They'll be adding olive oil to the kidney beans. A doctor will come to examine the prisoners. It's all planned. Transfer to the shacks. Transfer from the shacks.

Where to?

V.I.P. elucidates. From the shacks - to Poland. The other side is putting on pressure. The other side is angry. The other side is being beaten. On all fronts. It's not giving up on the Jews. Firm in its determination to exterminate them. To the very last one of them. The Bulgarian government has no objection. In principle. The Bulgarian government is prepared to send all camp inmates to the incinerators!..

V.I.P. is agitated. Shoulders quake.

V.I.P. weeps.

A V.I.P. weeping!

Strong impulse to reassure him.

This isn't definite! - he cries.

The proof is - I'm still here! It isn't definite!

A feather-light touch on the V.I.P.'s thick arm.

V.I.P. is more agitated than ever. His head, perched on the colossal neck of a classical statue, is quivering.

Pulls a handkerchief from the pocket of his trousers, which are clean and, wonder of wonders - pressed! Wipes eyes, nose, face. Quivering stops. Elephantine head, erect. Voice lucid.

There is a dispute going on between the overlord, demanding the lives of the Jews, and the vassal, under whose jurisdiction they live.

Overlord, vassal.

The vassal isn't prepared to meet the costs of

transportation. The overlord demands that the vassal meet the costs of transportation. Demands forcibly. A few days ago – by explicit order. Direct, unequivocal, unprecedented.

How will the vassal react?

The lives of the Jews. They are corralled in the concentration camp of Somovit. Two years ago, the vassal was ready and willing to do the job. To carry the costs of transportation. Two years ago there were victories. Quick victories, stunning, exciting, reassuring victories. Now, it's a different situation. All change. Instead of victories – ignominious defeat. The end is near. Anyone can see. The overlord will bear the consequences. The vassal... is in a panic. To this day, it has never refused the overlord anything. Not even the faintest hint of a refusal. Full compliance, in everything. To this very day. From this day onward – there will be changes.

The vassal is aware of the risks. Jewish lives – another indictment for the post-war tribunal. War crimes.

The costs of transportation.

The vassal still feels the pain of shelling out for the transportation of the Jews of Greece and Macedonia. Coffers are running low, a chronic haemorrhaging of funds. No way of making up the shortfall.

The vassal is defiant. The Jews – they're yours for the taking if you want them. The trains, the ships – not at our expense. Not ever! A point of principle.

Question:

Who is the one who will save the Jews of Bulgaria? A king? A people? Peter Denov?

Answer:

It's economics.

There is hope, Niso Makedonka smiles. There is hope, Niso Makedonka reassures himself.

V.I.P. on the verge of release. He's leaving. Asks a favour of the youngest of the Gavroches.

The youngest Gavroche is listening.

A thousand leva.

He'll lend the young Gavroche a thousand leva. Young Gavroche sits up, a dignified pose. Rags flapping on a pole. His voice cold, calm, resolute.

He won't accept it.

A loan! – Niso Makedonka insists.

No.

Where are all the non-rule rules of the camp?

He doesn't ask himself. His consciousness is clear. Not even the shadow of a thought. Not this way or that way. Not even a shadow of agonising over a decision. His mind is made up. The determination of an imprisoned Gavroche. Sub-animal.

Niso Makedonka has a letter addressed to him. From his mother. A short letter. To read and destroy. Reply on the paper provided. His reply will be delivered to its destination.

"My dear son" – his mother begins. He recognises her loose, eminently legible handwriting. His hand shakes. He can't stop the tears.

Niso Makedonka holds out a handkerchief. He wipes his face. "I'm doing everything I can to get you released... accept five hundred leva from the bearer. His wife received it from me. Hugs and kisses: Mother, Sister, Aunt."

Well? – asks Niso Makedonka. A note of triumph.

Did you read the letter? – he asks sternly.

No. My wife told me that she got five hundred leva

from your mother.

Not a thousand.

Not a thousand – his interlocutor confirms.

He accepts five hundred leva. Hard cash, legal tender.

Bread, cheese, maybe even – a pear. Grapes. Several days supply.

Five hundred leva!

A distant, pleasant warmth spreads over his cheeks. A memory of his childhood – surprised by a gift he had never expected to receive.

No regrets for missing out on a duty! – grins Niso Makedonka.

No.

Writes to his mother:

"Everything's fine. When you meet Niso Makedonka, you'll get to hear how reasonable the conditions are here – comfortable even. You'll see for yourself – the man has put on weight. Things will work out for the best, and soon. Best wishes to Sister, Aunt, all our other relations – and Dad, hoping that he'll soon be coming home from the labour camp."

Niso Makedonka beams. A broad, captivating, sincere smile.

They shake hands. A firm handshake. Strong impulse to embrace, which doesn't materialise. They both promise to themselves, and to each other, that they'll meet again after victory.

As a man is comforted by his mother, so shall I comfort you (Isaiah LXVI, 13).

Niso Makedonka, After

Wide-ranging activity in the service of the new regime.

Wide-ranging activity in the organisation of Jewish immigration to Israel.

An invitation to meet the Secretary of the Party. A man with an impressive past: underground, prison, Spain, Moscow, supervision and coordination of partisan units.

Vigorous, charismatic. A stalwart communist.

A cheery meeting, comfortable conversation. Tea and biscuits.

The Party Secretary: It is incumbent upon all supporters of the new administration to fulfil their obligations to the sacred cause of the Revolution. The objective justifies the way and the means. Any way whatsoever, any means whatsoever. The objective – to build a new world. A world of liberty and equality. Cleansed of superstition, rid of parasitism. The process requires sacrifice.

Niso Makedonka stiffens. The Party Secretary continues:

Niso Makedonka has a long-standing friend. A fervent Zionist. Zionism is to be denounced. The objective justifies the means. Niso Makedonka is to testify in court that his long-standing friend is an agent of Anglo-American espionage services. He will testify as to his criminal attempt to recruit him too, Niso Makedonka, into spying on behalf of the corrupt West, against the progress of the proletariat, over which no power in the world can prevail. Its victory is a self-evident fact, a historical imperative...

Niso Makedonka turns pale. In a faltering voice, he makes some totally spurious point, about evidence. He gets no response. The position is clear. There is nowhere he can go, no one he can convince, no one he can turn to.

The Party Secretary fixes gimlet-eyes on him, uncompromising, cold.

Silence.

Prolonged, awkward silence.

The Party Secretary reminds Niso Makedonka that he is father to a wonderful family. He counts them off, one by one: loyal wife, promising son, attractive daughter. Their future hangs in the balance. Is it his intention to destroy his children's future? Turn his family into outcasts, for the sake of some obsolete bourgeois prejudices? Will anyone be pleased to hear that his loyal wife - is the wife of a traitor, convicted by a people's court of serious crimes? That his promising son is the son of a father who passed state secrets to Anglo-American agents, in return for large sums of money? That his daughter, who has her heart set on a career in paediatric medicine, is the daughter of a man who betrayed the Party's trust, conspired to undermine and destabilise the regime of progress and equality - a spineless, bourgeois parasite?

A silence deeper than the pit of Hell.

The Party Secretary: he must give an answer.

Significant pause.

The Party Secretary: there is no doubt, a heavy responsibility rests on his shoulders.

Continuing, in a more conciliatory tone: A true fighter for progress does not shirk responsibility, however heavy it may be. He does not run away. He must prove that he is a genuine fighter for progress. He must prove that he is worthy to bear responsibility, making his contribution towards the final and decisive victory of socialism.

He must give an answer.

He's been given an opportunity.

To prove his loyalty to the socialist homeland.

He must give him an answer.

Within twenty-four hours, and not a minute more.

The Party Secretary rises to his feet.

The interview is over.

A handshake.

Cold as death.

Niso Makedonka leaves the newly-built, tastefully furnished tenement block that is Party headquarters.

A late spring day. Pleasantly, agreeably warm.

Niso Makedonka boards Tram Number 2.

Rides to the terminus. Old Jewish cemetery.

Niso Makedonka sits on a flattened tombstone, in the shade of a leafy tree. Takes a notebook from the inside pocket of his jacket, a ballpoint pen. Writes: "Let my wife, my son and my daughter, go to Israel!"

Three copies: one in his trouser pocket, another on the flattened tombstone, with a pebble to hold it down. The third – between his powerful neck and the belt, with which he hangs himself.

His strange weeping at the time of their parting.

He wept for himself.

The Party Secretary allows the widow of Niso Makedonka, the son of Niso Makedonka and the daughter of Niso Makedonka, to leave Bulgaria and emigrate to Israel. Niso Makedonka has paid the price. Paid in full.

Not by might nor by power but by my spirit (Zechariah IV, 6).

Revolution

Shlomo Kalo testifies:

Not long after my liberation from the concentration-camp, a revolution took place in my homeland and a new order held sway, imposing radical changes in human and in ideological terms. All those who remained loyal to the former regime, who only the day before yesterday were still bearing arms, were disarmed, denounced as traitors and instigators, arrested and imprisoned. Their weapons were transferred into the no less skilled hands of adherents to the new regime.

Without any advance planning, almost spontaneously and in a manner typical of all revolutions, a series of executions began immediately, carried out in the most economical manner possible. In the minds of the revolutionary leaders there were many burning questions, infinitely more important than the execution issue – administration and methodology. And in a departure from the practice of former revolutions, they progressed to the point of doing all their killing in secret, without a hint of the strident exhibitionism that is designed to inflame spirits and sow fear and unease.

It could be said that in this sense, the revolution was distinguished by a unique brand of cultural restraint, novel but hardly inspiring hope.

Early in the morning, the new bearers of arms would load onto commandeered trucks the previous owners of those arms and drive in haste, without undue commotion, to the suburbs of the capital city.

The faces of captors and captives alike were unshaven, and all showed the vestiges of sleepless nights. Sometimes the armed men exchanged glances with their anxious prisoners. There was no need for the medium of speech; the eyes of both parties expressed a kind of solitary, vacant resentment, against somebody or something – address unknown.

At the designated site, already waiting for them were the revolutionaries of the "technical branch", meaning those responsible for the maintenance of spades, shovels and hoes. As soon as the ones destined for slaughter had been unloaded, their hands were untied and each was given one of the tools supplied by the technicians. Sometimes, the free choice of the candidate for slaughter was exercised, sometimes it was down to the wisdom and perspicacity of a member of the technical team: for the weakling – a hoe, for the tough guy – a spade. Shovels were distributed among those who, in some way or another, had aroused the disgust or the ire of the team.

The work proceeded energetically, without anyone uttering a superfluous word. All were united, slaughterers and their prospective victims, in the one aim – to finish the job quickly, and for some reason – have it finished before sunrise. Usually, luck smiled on them, and all was done in time and to their complete satisfaction.

And if it was the case that one of the candidates for slaughter showed incompetence in his work, or was unsteady on his feet for some reason or another, a watchful member of the slaughterers' team would immediately take the digging implement from his hand and, without regard for his own dignity, help him out with his allotted task, energetically and in a spirit of friendly cooperation.

When the trench had attained reasonable proportions in the professional estimation of the experienced team-leaders, the signal was given. Without a word said, members of the "brigade" – comprising personnel of the technical branch and the prisoner-escort units – exercising totally free choice, would pick out for themselves one of the "candidates", lead him to the edge of the pit, place the muzzle of a loaded pistol against his temple, and without hesitation, before the man had time to moan and most important of all, before the first ray of sunlight appeared, squeeze the trigger.

The sound of the shot was muffled, reminiscent of the innocuous popping of a firework, like those used to mark revolutionary celebrations or the birthday of a leading apparatchik. The body, which just a few seconds before had been sweating profusely, wetting its crumpled trousers and shaking in every muscle, would fall where it stood, and make its slithering way, hesitant and ungainly, from the edge of the pit to the bottom.

And if it came about that, on account of some unhelpful movement, the corpse keeled over in the wrong direction, away from the pit, then it was the job of the responsible "team" or "brigade" member, to catch it in time and give it a vigorous shove in the opposite, desired direction, thus sparing himself the onerous task of dragging it to the bottom of the pit with his own hands.

When a member of the team or the brigade had finished with one "candidate" he immediately turned to the next, without hesitation and without the slightest inclination to shirk responsibility. In general, you could say that each one of these revolutionaries did a sterling job, clean and exemplary revolutionary work, and for this reason, despite the strict revolutionary rules which do not discriminate in favour of anyone, members of the brigade were not allocated specific quotas, so long as they continued to prove, incontrovertibly, that they were doing everything required of them to the best of their revolutionary conscience. And sure enough, within a relatively short time, the work was completed. The more energetic among the revolutionaries could expect incentive-bonuses and the posting of their names on the unit's notice-board. One team-leader even earned the honour of meeting the chairman of the Central Committee in the capital, and the latter awarded him the customary revolutionary commendations, finally parting from him with a fraternal pat on the shoulder and a firm handshake.

Anyone less adept at handling the process, and there were some such, leaving a corpse on the edge of the pit or outside it, could expect to hear a caustic comment from the leader of the team to which he belonged, and the order to go back at once and drag it to the bottom of the pit, with his own hands and without any assistance. In extricating himself he was expected to clear a path for himself through the piles of bodies, treading on them if necessary. These were fresh bodies, still twitching and even, as a result of some reflex process, which has yet to be examined in depth by the medical profession, turning on their sides and impeding his progress.

Sometimes, admittedly not often, one of the "candidates" would protest his innocence of any crime or misdemeanour, and express his total inability to understand why it was his fate to be slaughtered on this grey morning, about to descend upon the world in the full and majestic glory of the dawn, as it is every other morning, and will ever be...

No one bothered to answer such a man. It was forbidden anyway. Sometimes, and this happened even less often, someone would fall to his knees, in a futile attempt at prayer. This would be the cue for an alert team-member to demonstrate his loyalty and absolute dedication to the hallowed principles of the Revolution by running to the man and knocking him out of his kneeling position with a well-aimed kick, putting an end at once to this conspiracy to disrupt a proper revolutionary procedure with obsolete rituals, the very kind of superstitious nonsense that proved to the world the necessity of revolution in the first place.

The team-member would then shoot him without taking the precaution of putting the muzzle of the pistol to his temple, thus risking the waste of a precious revolutionary bullet. If by chance he missed the target or inflicted only injury, needing another bullet to complete the job, the price of the extra ammunition, plus a fine, would be deducted from his wages.

Shooting a kneeling man was singled out for special praise as an exemplary revolutionary act, showing efficiency as well as dedication to progressive principles. The bodies of those shot on their knees outside the pit were at least accorded the privilege of four pall-bearers apiece from among the candidates for slaughter, and if there were not enough of them left for this, or if those who were left were incapable of it, there would always be blank-faced volunteers from the ranks of the committed revolutionaries present, especially the younger ones among them.

Among the candidates for slaughter there were some who, a few seconds before the hot muzzle of the pistol was put to their heads, would hurriedly pull from their pockets an ornament or a watch, "a family memento, of purely sentimental value", and offer it to the one on the point of squeezing the trigger. The latter would twist his face into a leer of ostentatious contempt, take without a word the object offered to him, and before putting a bullet in the head of his benefactor, hand it over to the team leader who would hastily register it as a contribution to the official fund for "Progress of the Revolution and its Sacred Goals".

Any team member who behaved otherwise would be expelled from the Party there and then, his red notebook would be confiscated, and his dossier marked, in red ink, with the single word "Unreliable" – resulting in his rapid dispatch to a labour camp for an indefinite period of "Re-education". According to eye-witnesses and financial commissars, such cases were exceedingly rare, and could be counted on the fingers of a pair of hands. In this way the purity of the revolutionary enterprise was maintained, and its hallowed principles saved from contamination.

Another topic requiring consideration in these circumstances was the bloodstains. Fragments of brain tissue, flying in every conceivable direction, were apt to land on heavy canvas jerkins and smartly pressed linen jackets. Equally exposed to staining were shirts, trousers, hats of various kinds, sandals and shoes and needless to say, the exposed, unshaven faces and the hands of those holding the pistols. As there was no official statement of guidelines to be followed in such circumstances, team-members had to use their own initiative, their wealth of experience and their talent for improvisation. Those who didn't trust in miracles resorted to thick rubber aprons, of the kind worn by meat-cutters in abattoirs. Others, unable to afford such aprons, took great care not to be caught too close at hand when a skull was penetrated by a bullet, either on the "entry" side or the "exit" side. And there were some who used pistols of miniature calibre, 6.35 mm, capable of perforating a human skull on one side only, causing no "exit" wound, and they protected themselves from the "entry" wound with a round piece of cardboard, about 40 cm in diameter and with a hole in the middle, through which the muzzle of the gun could be poked during firing.

Anyway, the Revolution made no allowance for clothing ruined in the performance of a duty, however quintessentially revolutionary that duty might be, so it was incumbent upon members of the Brigade to beware of these bloody fragments of brain tissue, flying over implausible distances and landing in the most unexpected places. The story was told of a team-member who looked up, anxiously scanning the morning sky as it paled towards the dawn, and a sliver of brain tissue lodged in his nostril; a doctor had to extract it with a long pair of tweezers. Another unfortunate fellow took a blast of fresh brain debris in his left eye, causing irreparable contamination; after prolonged and ineffective treatment it was eventually replaced by a glass one.

Because I had fought alongside the revolutionaries against the dark scourge of the swastika – I was called upon to play my part in the consolidation of victory.

At sixteen years old, I was placed in command of a group of prisoners, most if not all of whom were due to make the short journey to the misty suburbs of the capital, before day-break.

To my great shame and to the revolutionary dissatisfaction, covertly or openly expressed, of my superiors, and after a miserable twenty-four hours of experience, I asked to be relieved of this duty. I excused my request on the grounds that I needed to return to my studies, and I hinted to my superiors that refusal of my application would not deter me from the foolhardy and supremely counter-revolutionary act of absconding – desertion in other words. I gambled everything on this one throw of the dice – and it paid off. I was discharged.

During that brief and tense period of time, a young man came to see me, a partisan, whose elder brother had been hanged on a dubious charge of disseminating subversive revolutionary material, under the laws of the previous regime. The man who actually hanged him, it emerged, was detained in the section for which I was responsible.

The young man, who had not yet turned twenty, came into the tiny office that I occupied, and demanded the hangman be brought from his cell.

When he saw the questioning look in my eyes, his stern demeanour eased a little and he explained, emphasising every word, how this hangman, not content with conventional strangulation, had grabbed his brother's legs as he was hanging and swung from them, bringing the full weight of his bulky frame to bear.

I had the hangman brought out.

He was a very tall man, his angular, balding head fringed by tufts of hair as black as pitch. His eyes were black, his dense beard black, as was his suit, black as the depths of Hell. He wore no shirt under his jacket; it seemed his arrest had caught him unawares.

With just one quick glance he realised which way things were going. Despite the shackles binding his wrists and ankles, and the chains attached to them, he fell, crouching at the feet of the young man, who was brandishing a sten-gun, and began kissing them fervently. The latter responded with a kick, but the former hangman was not deterred; he wiped the blood from his lips and resumed his kissing of the young man's muddy shoes.

While he was doing this, he was suddenly assailed by a fit of strange sounding hiccups and began weeping, floods of tears splashing on the shoes and on the floor, to the accompaniment of the indifferent, metallic clanging of the chains. After a few more kicks, the bereaved brother ordered the man kissing his shoes to stand up.

He obeyed and rose to his feet, his whole body shaking, convulsed by the hiccups, and the tears flowing into his beard and dripping to the floor, at a slow, heavy tempo.

The young man ordered him to lift his head and look him in the eyes. Surprisingly, the man in black refused to do this, continuing to hiccup, to sob and to shake, but resisting all efforts to make him look up, in spite of the obvious danger facing him.

The young man slapped his pale, fleshy cheek, and the hangman tried to kiss the hand that struck him, with utterly repulsive zeal.

For a long moment the young man stood motionless, frozen.

Clearly, if he wanted to, he could have taken aim and fired the sten-gun there and then – an abrupt end to the hiccups, the convulsions of the huge body and the choked weeping of a cowering animal.

As the "officer responsible" I had no choice but to witness the scene, repellent though it was. It took a lot of effort to control the nausea that was churning up my guts.

The young man made a move to unsling the automatic weapon from his shoulder, and the former hangman promptly fell prostrate at his feet with a clanking of chains, and proceeded to lick his shoes and the floor.

Again the peremptory order to stand up was heard, and the hangman obeyed with some effort, weighed down as he was by the heavy chains. Again the young man tried to catch a glimpse of the eyes of the prisoner, still shaking and sobbing, and the latter turned them away hastily, stubbornly, and having no other option – closed them.

And then, suddenly, the youth spat in the bearded face of the hangman, and with an abrupt movement, as if this was his way of blotting him out, once and for all, from his consciousness, he turned his broad back on him and walked away without a backward glance. His rhythmic footsteps reverberated in the gloom of the long, narrow corridor, until they faded into silence.

The hangman was taken back to his cell.

This conclusion, however pointless and repugnant it may have seemed, did me the favour of making my choices a great deal easier. I left that place with the firm determination never to return and sure enough, as previously mentioned, so it was.

And I will give you a new heart and put into you a new spirit, and take the stony heart out of your flesh (Ezekiel XXXVI, 26).

Shacks

Transfer to the shacks cancels out a day's work. It turns out that family types have a lot of baggage: suitcases, of every variety and size, stuffed full to overflowing, holdalls, baskets, knapsacks. Gavroches, whose personal loads amount to no more than the rags flapping on their skeletal bodies, are hired to carry the possessions of the familials. Prices are soaring. A suitcase and a knapsack - one hundred leva.

A steep hill, overlooking the Danube to the north, the hamlet of Somovit to the south, rises to an altitude of seven hundred metres.

The column of variegated freight shuffles along at a laborious pace. Gavroches improvise. Sticks are threaded through the handles of suitcases, hoisted in pairs across the shoulders and thus leaving the hands free for additional loads of bags and packages. The owners of the property walk alongside, panting as they issue incessant instructions to their porters, warning them to take the utmost care and avoid any incautious movement, any risk of damage to the cargo.

Scarface, hired by a middle-aged couple, owners of a haberdashery shop, who are constantly bitching and complaining about the exorbitant fee that he has charged, turns and sheds the load at their feet, warning the Gavroches that anyone touching the bags of the haberdashery couple will complete his journey to the shacks on a stretcher.

The bags are left abandoned on the roadway, dumped on bare ground like stones forever unturned. The couple are forced to drag them up the steep hill relying on their own resources, a process accompanied by constant and acrimonious bickering which can have only one outcome: divorce after victory.

Late at night the couple arrive at the shacks, their voices gone, feet stumbling, hands shaking, eyes streaming tears. The look on their faces: profound resentment of their betrayal, total betrayal, at the hands of the human race.

The shacks are new, whitewashed. A fresh smell of pine wood. An extensive building, with bunks in two shelves ranged along the wall. An upper shelf, a lower shelf. The floor – compressed earth.

Persistent rumour: the Bulgarian government is trying to change its image. The Bulgarian government sniffs the disaster approaching. The end. As in World War One. As it always has been, always will be.

The Bulgarian government is attached to the Teutons, devoted to the Teutons. Identifies with them. Teutonic asperity, Teutonic rigidity, Teutonic pedantry. Teutonic catastrophe. The Bulgarian government hasn't studied the past, hasn't drawn conclusions, hasn't learned the lesson required of it. Hasn't seen what's brewing. Total identification. Blindness of heart.

The Bulgarian government is trying to change its image.

At the last moment?

The Bulgarian government will pay the heavy price in full.

The Bulgarian government is in a panic.

Needs a change of image, urgently, desperately.

Change of image.

Partial. As partial as possible.

With no tangible effect, as per usual.

Let's start with the Jews.

Softening up. In all senses of the expression.

Shacks instead of huts. Olive oil in the bean soup.

Post.

Parcels.

Clothing – as supplied by the Jewish communities outside the camp.

A doctor.

For the first time since the camp was set up, a doctor comes calling. Young, inexperienced.

A long line.

The doctor is bashful. Has no idea what's expected of him, or even where he is. Refers two geriatrics to the hospital.

No place for Jews in a Bulgarian hospital.

The two old men taken back to the camp. Released.

Happy.

Both are suffering from cancer.

Both are happy.

Taking leave of their former hut-mates.

Not one of the Gavroches has complained of malnutrition. Not one of the geriatrics has complained of malnutrition, not one of the familials has complained of malnutrition.

Young, bashful, inexperienced doctor. Doesn't diagnose any cases of malnutrition. Not one of the inmates of the camp has complained of malnutrition.

Young, bashful, inexperienced doctor, goes back the way he came.

The camp remains as it was.

Without V.I.P.s
Gavroches, geriatrics, familials.
Not going out to work.

Saint Gregory, of the Fourteenth Century, goes on to say: "Do not be frivolous in your mind, and do not be carried away by the sight of your eyes. Be rational in your opinions, examine everything with the greatest care, cling to the good and shun the bad. You should always consider and examine, and only thereafter – believe."

Old Haim

Old Haim is stressed, anxious, scared. Of release. He likes the shack. The clothes he's received from the community - he likes those too. The bread ration hasn't changed but they say it's going to change, go up to a full half-kilo. Olive oil in the bean soup. Extra beans too - between ten and twelve to a dish. More goodies on the way.

Haim has no family. None whatsoever. He has nowhere to go, no one to turn to. Distant relatives shun him, beware of him. Detest the idea of taking him in, having to support him. They insist, they don't know him. Insist there are no blood-ties between them. No relationship whatsoever. He's not a man like them. Not a Jew like them. Not young like them. A troublesome old man, not wanted.

He has nowhere to go. No one to turn to. Nothing to do. He'll die in the street, like an abandoned dog. Die of hunger, die of grief.

The shack is preferable. For all kinds of reasons, innumerable reasons. Decidedly preferable. Haim is assailed by a mounting sense of fear, abject fear. Fear of death.

Two weeks.

Two more geriatrics released. Smiles, handshakes, felicitations, happiness.

Haim is fearful, anxious, stressed, depressed.

He'll refuse to be released.

Won't budge from the shack.

When they call his name, he won't answer. They'll take the release-order back to the centre. In the capital, faraway. Record him as "non-existent". Forget him. That's what laconic in-his-forties says, and he's seen everything, experienced everything, knows everything.

Best to stay in the shack. Not descend into the chaotic morass of the outside world. Not be exposed to arrogance and hatred.

Haim feels more at ease. A distant, hesitant smile, rising on wizened face. Wrinkles are smoothed.

A smile giving limpid clarity to old Haim's features, purity to his eyes. Eyes of an infant.

Haim feels more at ease.

Thanks to laconic in-his-forties.

Thanks to the ever prescient advice of laconic in-his-forties.

Haim's parents died when he was a child.

He grew up in an orphanage.

Worked as a licensed market porter. Made a respectable living. Married a wife. No children. He wanted children, wanted them very much. His wife went for tests. Unequivocal, medical diagnosis: sterility, permanent. Conception impossible.

And that's official.

No children. He gets used to the idea. His wife has three brothers and a sister. They don't think much of their brother-in-law. "Backward," they call him. Their children don't visit his house.

The wife of Haim the porter falls ill. Tuberculosis. Three brothers and a sister blame Haim for her sickness. The wife of Haim the porter dies, gives up the ghost. No more wife.

The brothers and sister of his late wife, spurn Haim their brother-in-law, treating him like a stranger, an alien.

His strength begins to fail him. At the age of sixty, he gives up portering. Takes a job as a waiter. At the age of seventy, dismissed. Too slow. Too slow for his employer, too slow for the customers.

Ventures out into a strange and dark world, without a cent in his pocket.

Rents himself a dilapidated hut in an even more dilapidated backyard. For a whole year, pays no rent. Before he can be evicted from his accommodation, the authorities arrest him.

Concentration camp.

Gavroches-geriatrics.

One hundred and forty grams of bread per day. Warm, salty water. Six to eight kidney beans. Dialogue with violent Gavroches. Kicks. Punches.

To be freed. Doesn't think about the future. Doesn't plan.

To be freed.

Better to die in the street than die here. To die like an abandoned dog – at liberty.

Not here.

Shacks. Thoughts of outside.

Better to stay.

Old Haim.

Old Haim, after.

The shacks are emptied. Half a dozen geriatrics sprawl on a shelf, that used to accommodate two dozen prisoners.

Rations are adequate. Guards friendly. Only five left. Release is at hand.

Local gang of fascist youths torches the shacks. Fire-fighters are joined by volunteers from the township, to extricate the old men. Haim refuses to be rescued, rejects the outstretched hands, retreats into the flames.

Old Haim.

The end.

Temujin.

Born 1155 or 1162, near Lake Beikal, Mongolia. Died 18. 8. 1227. Known by his title of Genghis Khan, meaning "Ruler of the World" in the Mongolian language.

Thirteenth Century historian Matthew Paris describes the Mongols, under the leadership of Genghis Khan as: "The detested race of Satan, who rose like devils from the deepest pit of Hell, from Tartarus, whence they are rightly know as Tartars."

Unanimously dubbed a genius, in celebration of his exceptional talents, expressed as they were in a single and unique way: consistent and unremitting slaughter of whole peoples, races, nations, until not a trace of them was left. Meticulous and thorough erasure, over the whole face of the earth, of prosperous settlements, burgeoning cities, thriving enterprises, of every kind and magnitude, till they turned into desert and ruin.

Laconic in-his-forties, After

Joins the revolutionaries.

In recognition of his persecution at the hands of the previous regime, and in accordance with his professional talents, offered a post in the accounts administration department of a collective steel works. Turns it down.

Applies for a job in the capital city's sanitation services.

Taken on.

Sweeps the streets.

Satisfactory performance. Promoted. Responsible for sanitation services in his home district.

Lives with a woman working in a cigarette factory.

Despite all his efforts to keep a low profile, his abilities are appreciated. Another promotion offer: supervisor of sanitation for the southern sector of the capital.

Rejects it.

Efforts to persuade him.

Refuses.

Threats.

Digs his heels in.

Refusal accepted.

At the age of sixty, abandons his life-partner, emigrates to Israel. Dies on the way there. Heart-attack.

Mistaken for a Zionist campaigner of wide repute, a valiant opponent of the communist regime.

Buried with full national honours on Mount Scopus, Jerusalem, under somebody else's name. Laconic in-his-forties.

True servants of God will worship the Father in spirit and in truth, for the Father takes pleasure in such worship. God is a spirit, and those who worship him, must worship in spirit and in truth (St. John's Gospel, IV, 23-24).

The Fortune-Teller

A middle-aged guard, a married man, the one who, before the move to the shacks, approached him with the offer of washing the guards' dishes in return for superior scraps of food, is wandering about mournfully, perplexed.

Rumour has it: his wife has fallen ill. An appeal for leave rejected out of hand. Sergeant-major vetoes it, camp commandant vetoes it.

Middle-aged guard, married man, walks about the camp consumed by anxiety, in deep dejection.

Staring, hollow look.

The pickpocket is clearing out rubbish from the new shack, collides with the guard, dropping a pile of empty boxes. Recoils in terror, expecting a kick. Middle-aged guard, married man, stoops without thinking, helps him pick them up.

A fresh batch of prisoners.

A woman in her fifties. Green, piercing eyes, expressing, in normal times, dismissive superiority, in the camp – hysteria. Hair, which until the other day was meticulously coifed, appropriately dyed, is revealed to all eyes in its demeaning, ruthless greyness. Colourful dress, like a gypsy's dress, which until the other day lent an air of mystery to the one who wore it, hangs down limply, shapeless and crumpled, a pitiable sight.

A woman lacking style, deprived of her dignity, on

the verge of unseemly collapse. Profession: clairvoyant. Of high renown, intimidating. Until the other day.

Crammed into a corner, on the lower shelf near the door, exposed to potentially lethal draughts. Mixed quarters.

On the firm advice of the camp pickpocket, the middle-aged guard, married man, on the verge of breakdown, approaches the fortune-teller. Maybe she can help, maybe she can offer ease to an aching heart.

Middle-aged guard, married man, arrives at the shack with its mixed-sex population, approaches the fortune-teller.

Silence.

Deep, loaded, tangible.

In a magisterial, imperious voice, that has not yet lost its hollow authority, the highly respected gentleman is invited to sit on the edge of the bench, hold out both his hands.

No one moves. No one stirs.

The fortune-teller is taking a risk. If her predictions fail to materialise, all the humiliations she can possibly imagine will be as nothing compared with what is bound to befall her.

The fortune-teller knows. The shack, with its two shelves, filled to overflowing, knows. Married, middle-aged, dejected guard knows.

Cold penetrates bones and hearts. Perhaps, the fortune-teller will rise, admit with total honesty that she has nothing to say, declare that her entire profession is nothing more than innocent make-believe, harmless deceit.

Two square, calloused hands, of a peasant by birth, who chose to join the prison service, are held out.

This peasant-guard can't be expected to display a highly developed sense of humour, waive his dignity and leave the shack smiling, in jovial mood.

The fortune-teller with the tormented look, still retaining some scraps of confidence, is well aware of the predicament into which she has propelled herself.

She utters a loud, piercing and carefully modulated shriek, like an invocation of spirits or the conjuring of a familiar, intended for the ears of the other inhabitants of the shack, looking on in stunned silence – those of them who understand Ladino, which the guard does not:

"Tell me something about him!"

From the shelf above a hollow cry is heard: "*La mujer esta hazina* – His wife is sick."

The fortune-teller sighs with relief.

Her bowed back straightens. She is a plant on the point of withering, granted, at the last moment, an invigorating dose of water.

With measured, practised movements, she takes into her ageing hands the heavy hands of the peasant-guard. Casts her eyes down, scrutinising minutely every line, every crevice. Over some of them she passes a long-nailed finger, which in the not so distant past was manicured and treated with purple lacquer, and is now astonishingly dirty, with a stratum of mud encrusted under the cracked nail.

Words drop from parched lips, rolling out one after the other in remarkable order, with measured pauses. Clear, crafted words, not susceptible to any misunderstanding.

Someone is lying on a bed.

Someone close – a wife perhaps.

She can't identify the sex.

A beloved family member, lying on a bed. Sick.

A pause. Deep, awesome. All the strings of the listener's soul are wound up to the highest possible tension. Liable to snap, at any moment. Fixed stare of emerald eyes coming back to life, radiating mysterious light. Unshakable confidence.

She has a message for him.

A true message, as follows:

He is to dismiss worry from his heart! An order, not to be disobeyed. This close relative, this dear and precious person, will rise from the sickbed. Will be well again. Will make a full and rapid recovery! That is all!

The guard rises, stunned. Bows emphatically. Leaves with a spring in his step. Returns. With awe and deference presents to the fortune-teller, the all-knowing oracle, from whom no secret is hidden, fresh bread, cheese, two pears. Bows again, without saying a word. Leaves the shack.

The fortune-teller swoops on the bread, cheese, pears. She gobbles with gusto, withered cheeks set to burst. She has no intention of sharing with anyone. This is all for her.

The one who saved the situation makes his voice heard again. Demands his fee. She breaks off a tiny morsel of bread, a minute lump of cheese. He devours them,

demands more.

The fortune-teller glowers. Her "familiar" glowers. He gestures with his eyes towards the outside. He will go out. He will tell. He has every right to go out and tell. Reveal the truth. At this very moment. He wants half the bread, half the cheese, a pear.

He gets them.

A former bank manager turns to the fortune-teller. What happens if the condition of the wife deteriorates and if, God forbid, she passes away?

The fortune-teller replies, while munching noisily:

He will realise there is nothing to be done, he will understand he has been given the one thing he desired more than anything else – a little reassurance. In his heart of hearts, every person longs for a little reassurance. In hard times. In his hard times. Scholar and idiot, fool and savant alike.

She slows the pace of her chewing.

Close cooperation between victim and predator, between exploiter and exploited, between desperate guard and charlatan clairvoyant. The guard needs the charlatan, the charlatan needs the guard. They give to one another what they want from one another. Food – for the charlatan, words of reassurance – for the guard. Each receives from the other what he longs to receive.

"Dispel resolutely any suspicion that arises in your heart against any person whomsoever. It is suspicion that puts an end to peace and love. Accept any suffering that befalls you with fortitude, since suffering gives to you the opportunity to grow in sublime patience, which paves the way to the truth". (Theoleptus of Philadelphia, Fourteenth Century).

Potatoes

Time brings changes to fruition.
Past, present, future.
Arrest. Interrogation. Camp. Stone buildings in the outskirts of a town. Shacks on the slope of a bare hill. Stunning view. The cold is stunning too. As is the hunger.
The camp pickpocket.
A youth of seventeen. Fingers of a virtuoso pianist. Rubber body of a circus acrobat. Intellect sharper than a razor blade.
Time brings changes to fruition.
The camp pickpocket has an idea.
How to soften potatoes. How to turn a live potato into an edible potato. How to eat it with gusto, thereby helping the potato to fulfil its destiny - to be eaten. Stuff oneself with potatoes.
Ingenious idea.
Ingenious plan.
Part A: Three to four potatoes of average size to be liberated from the cart. He is responsible for the implementation of Part A.
Part B - this being the full responsibility of the camp pickpocket - the potatoes selected from the sack on the guards' supply cart to be placed at his disposal.
Empty ration tin. Just the right size. Three to four potatoes in it, plus sufficient water to cover them. Lid. Fire.
Secluded corner, protected from the winds. Protected from the eyes of the guards, protected from the prying eyes of prisoners. Wait for the right

moment.

Empty ration tin. Four potatoes in it, with enough water to cover them. Tin lid, enclosing the container and its contents with a hermetic seal. A thick piece of wood, shaped like a whip, threaded through matching holes on top of the lid, holding it in place and increasing the pressure. Quick cooking – the pressure-cooker principle.

Ready?

Ready.

Stage by stage, the plan is converted from theory into practice.

Secluded corner at the edge of the camp. A narrow circle of stones on which the tin of potatoes is placed. Beneath it, wood-shavings, twigs, sawdust. The one responsible for Part B has a matchbox in his possession – containing three live matches.

Fire.

Lively, reassuring.

Excited looks. Nothing compares with the happiness of friends joining together to dine on fresh, cooked potatoes.

The rich, nourishing taste, healthy, invigorating.

No point sitting around the little campfire. No point arousing suspicion.

Better to go away, for a few minutes.

Down to the shacks. Pent-up anticipation on the point of overflowing. Needs to be restrained.

Just for a few minutes.

There's no hurry.

No need to be impatient.

A loud explosion shatters the pastoral calm of the

camp.

A mortar.

Artillery.

High explosive.

Sabotage.

Partisans are storming the camp. To free their oppressed brothers. To bring the oppressors to justice.

Panic-stricken guards running hither and thither, in frantic circles. Gleaming Schmeisers loaded, at the ready.

Partisans have no mercy.

Better to fold and flee.

Guards terrified to the marrow of their bones. Faces show expressions of craven supplication, cringing servility, appeal for mercy. Finger on the trigger of the Schmeiser.

Open fire or not?

Against whom?

If these are partisans – there are only two choices, shoot to kill or – escape.

Escape.

Partisans and those who will come after them are good at bearing grudges. Partisans and those who will come after them are intent on vengeance. No one will escape from their hand.

Guards scurrying this way and that, in every possible direction. Hands sweating on the trigger of the gleaming Schmeiser.

The pickpocket shouts: "The potatoes!"

Run to the hiding-place.

Exposed to the view of all. Visible to the guards too.

No tin. No lid. No threaded stick. No potatoes. No sign of the catering effort on an improvised barbecue – pressure-cooker principle.

Eye-witnesses describe a strange bright object seen at the time of the explosion, hurtling into the sky, fading away and disappearing as if it had never existed.

Potatoes have turned into mash. Puree. Puree is raining down, landing on the grass over a wide radius.

A moment of hesitation, the next – swooping on the grass, licking up the puree that has stuck to it.

Standing up.

Trying to stand. On the head of each of them, three automatic weapons are trained. On the faces of the armed men – bewilderment. Mounting anger, blazing hatred. Lust for revenge. A desperate effort to cover up the shame, the fear, the helplessness, the loss of nerve.

Sergeant-major arrives. Interrogation on the spot. Precise details.

An irrational smile twists the face of the sergeant-major. Six guards escorting two Gavroches. Automatic weapons at the ready.

No more surprises.

The news spreads with the speed of thought. They all know. Guards know, prisoners know. All the camp knows. All of it. Down to the tiniest, the microscopic details.

Prisoners are nervous. They're going to be punished. Severe, collective punishment. They shall see and they shall fear. Two foolhardy Gavroches are jeopardising the welfare of all the prisoners. The culprits should be thrashed till they're senseless, thrashed till they're no longer recognisable – they could be Chinese, Japanese, Indian. They should be thrashed till they snuff it.

Collective punishment.

Must organise a delegation. Report to the camp commandant, the sergeant-major, the guards, disown the two Gavroches. Plead for mercy, compassion, forgiveness. Grovel in the dust. Promise that never, never, never will anything like this happen again! Older inmates will keep a close eye on those frivolous, mischievous tearaways, habitual criminals...

They are led to the guards' new quarters, automatic weapons still aimed at their backs, prodding them.

Everything's clear. To the last detail.

A full report has been received on the theft of four potatoes of average size from the guards' food store. Stealing the guards' food – no punishment can atone for that.

The explosion!

Clear criminal intent. Clear as crystal.

They planned all this.

With the intention of causing mass panic, disorder, loss of nerve. They're acting on instructions from outside. Red Army, partisans. Their conspiracy has failed. It was doomed to failure from the start.

Solemn procession.

The guards who arrested: satisfaction soaring sky-high, pride beyond measure. Gavroches who were arrested: satisfaction soaring sky-high, pride beyond measure.

Inside their spotlessly clean quarters, the guards

make haste to lay on the gleaming pine wood table, with scrupulous neatness, four whips. Between each whip and its neighbour a carefully measured space. It must be possible to wield four whips simultaneously, without them snagging on one another or hindering one another.

Each Gavroche has two guards ministering to him.

They will all take part. To dispel the tension, anger, fear, frustration.

With or without whips. Everything taken into consideration.

There's no knowing if they'll come out of this still breathing. No way of knowing.

If they do come out of it – it won't be with the use of their own arms and legs, not with their own eyes and their own entrails, not with...

Broken machinery.

All the days of their lives.

Two revolting old men. One aged fifteen, the other – seventeen. Abhorred by humanity, abhorred by the world, abhorred by themselves.

Guards pace back and forth. Pleasurable anticipation.

The darkest cellar of the Inquisition would be a hundred times brighter than the guards' quarters in this camp, flooded with limpid light as they are.

Air.

Loaded.

Compressed.

Hate.

Vengeance.

Pleasure.

Murder.

Last moments.

Their last moments.

Looking into one another's eyes.

Instead of a handshake.

Everything's erased: fear, hate, anxiety, stress, mockery, resentment, cynicism, pride, happiness, insanity. Everything.

Consciousness clear, sharp, incisive. Facts. Acceptance of facts. Submission.

If allowed, they would have shaken hands.

All at once, four guards pick up four whips. Without an order. Acting on channelled inspiration. Telepathy.

Sergeant-major enters.

Hush.

Without advancing towards them he gives the order:

"Release them."

Weary voice. Almost indifferent. Authority, allowing for neither subtraction nor addition.

"Release them."

No exclamation mark, no additions.

Whips are put back on the table. With a rhythmic, synchronised movement, in the same order.

Sergeant-major goes out.

Release.

Fresh air. Sharp, dazzling light. Blessing of endless skies.

They don't believe, they refuse to believe the evidence of their senses.

The ground has fallen away from beneath their feet.

They are walking in an empty void. Processes frozen, machinery paralysed, thought fettered, heart melting, soul in deep shock.

A long moment.

Return to what was.

Processes, machinery, limbs, thought, heart, soul.

Return to what was.

The pickpocket puts a question:

What was that?

God – he tells him.

The pickpocket grimaces. He doesn't get it, refuses to get it. Guards don't get it, refuse to get it. Sergeant-major doesn't get it, refuses to get it. Prisoners don't get it, refuse to get it. Humanity doesn't get it, refuses to get it. The world doesn't get it, refuses to get it.

Saint John Climacus, of the Seventh Century, declares: "An open wound will not become worse and spread, but will be cured."

Sarika

The overlord gives the vassal land. The vassal gives the overlord Jews. Long, black, speeding trains. Crammed with Jews. Gobbling up the kilometres of track. Heart of Europe. Poland. Extermination camps.

Jews of Thrace and Macedonia.

Living on their land for the past fifteen hundred years. Conquerors come, conquerors are conquered, fade away and disappear as if they never were. The Jews stay.

Jews of Thrace and Macedonia. Deep roots.

Uprooted.

Crammed into horse-wagons.

Man, woman, boy, girl, infant, crone.

Trains crammed to overflowing. Crossing the whole width of Bulgaria, from end to end. Impatient, angry, gobbling up the kilometres, leaving behind them a heavy pall of black, viscid smoke, refusing to disperse. Black trains. Trains of death.

The Jews of Thrace. The trains of Hell nearing the end of the line. Death in the furnaces of Poland.

No water for the prisoners, no facilities for those crammed into horse-wagons. No air.

The Jewish communities of Bulgaria offer their services. Experienced cringers, with years of practice in the arts of servility, the giving of backhanders.

Permission is granted to provide water at remote stations. Also, prisoners may leave the trains for ablutions-breaks.

A moment – release from suffocation. A moment – freedom from the tyranny of time. A moment – away from the inferno.

Giant brass taps, turned on. A steady stream. Pressing forward, drinking, splashing faces. Water drips from straggling, unruly hair and beards. They fill containers: jugs, bottles, water-bottles, pans, dishes. Then, a frenzied run to the toilets. Cramming into the stifling cubicle of an ancient latrine. Two and three at a time.

Vile stench of excrement. Fresh excrement. Urine floods the cubicle.

That's enough. Make room for a wife, a girl, an aged father, a mother with the seal of death stamped on her pale face, a grandchild...

Running back and forth, back and forth. Just long enough – to urinate, defecate, return to the wagon. Back to the crush of bodies, the suffocation. Back to Hell.

Not all of them.

The last one is still there, in the stinking cubicle.

The one who doesn't despise life, defects from the death train.

The one who doesn't despise the stench, is standing up to the challenge.

The one who can cope with living, defects from the death train.

The one who can cope with the stench, is standing up to the challenge.

The train emits a last, impatient, piercing whistle. Wagons rattle

Pressure of bodies destined for incineration.

Rushing towards the flames, yearning for the end.
The drop-out – stays.

Sarika.
Drop-out from the train.
Entrusted to the care of the Jewish community.
The Jewish community isn't interested in her. The
elite members of the community aren't interested in
her. The elders of the community aren't interested in
her.
They're not interested in Sarika. Half a dozen
drop-outs – yes. Sarika – no.
The leaders of the community ask questions.
The elders of the community ask questions.
The community asks questions.
Place of birth?
Sarika: Salonika.
Age?
Sarika: Eighteen.
Occupation?
Sarika: Whore. From the age of fourteen.
Until now.
Sarika is sent to a concentration camp, with the
agreement of all relevant parties. To the shacks.

Sarika, eighteen years of age. Low forehead, clear
eyes. Body – Astarte at her best. No fabric, however
coarse it might be, lacking individual style, worn,
faded, could blur to the slightest degree the fine
contour lines of Sarika's divine body. No fabric,
however coarse it might be, lacking individual style,
worn, faded, could blunt even symbolically the fine
contour lines of Sarika's divine body. Wherever Sarika
is, the air is electrified, fire blazes and the inferno

rages. No man in the world could stand before Sarika with indifference.

Sarika. Somovit concentration camp. Shacks. She finds space in the corner, at the end of the upper shelf. Among the familials. The surviving womenfolk form a barrier between her and their husbands.

Hunger stifles any spark of sexual desire, of any variety whatsoever, of any intensity whatsoever. Hunger of the huts.

Hunger of the shacks. Hunger-not-hunger.

Sarika: body of a goddess, eyes of a saint, face of a retard.

Sarika: hell-fire. Electric shock.

She's not giving her favours to anyone. Flirting with her – a waste of time. Flirters get short shrift from her.

No equivocation, no compromise.

Sarika doesn't give favours to prisoners.

She's not attracted to Jews.

Sarika consorts with guards. Men in uniform turn her on.

Uproar in the shacks.

Gavroches threatening to revolt.

"Lynch Sarika!"

Laconic in-his-forties doesn't object. Scarface – incensed. Scarface is a volcano on the point of erupting. Fire and lava.

Scarface demands an explanation.

There's no avoiding Scarface.

No one who values his life will try to avoid giving an explanation to Scarface.

Sarika values her life She's not taking any risks.

Scarface confronts Sarika. He - taut as a bow-string, she - sitting calmly in her corner on the shelf.

Scarface demands an explanation.

The evening is young. The upper shelf is tense, all agog. The lower shelf is tense, all agog. All the blazing eyes of the occupants of both shelves are fixed on Sarika. Fury, indignation, hate, resentment, irresistible lust. Spite. Lynch Sarika!

Scarface demands an explanation. The whole shack demands an explanation. Gavroches who have come into the shack demand an explanation. Looks that bode nothing good. Dark, heavy, ready for anything.

Sarika owes them an explanation. Why is it "yes" to the guards, but "no" to her partners in destiny?

The stillness before the storm.

Sarika has no problem explaining. She doesn't avoid explanations. She isn't a liar by nature. Sincere as only a whore can be, sincere as only a saint can be, sincere as only a retard can be, as only a great soul can be.

She has syphilis. Highly infectious.

Tension eases. Eyes are lowered. A hefty portion of shame. Sighs of relief.

Occupants of the lower shelf draw back, huddling together and drawing in their heads like tortoises. Occupants of the upper shelf avert their gaze. No one looks at his neighbour. No one looks at Sarika. Gavroches are silent. For a moment. The next, they turn and leave Sarika's shack.

Scarface's head is bowed. He's thinking something through, taking his time over it. His head is lifted again.

A look of empathy in his eyes.

Those who know Scarface have never seen him with a look of empathy in his eyes. They would never imagine him capable of an empathic look. Scarface extends a huge, blacksmith's hand. She places in it, cautiously, the warm hand of an eighteen year old girl.

Well done! - Scarface intones, then turns and leaves the shack.

Sarika.

Afterwards - no information.

The end - no information.

Saint Simeon, of the Tenth-Eleventh Century, declares: "If the obedience of a pupil to his spiritual master is complete, he will be freed from all fear and oppression. It is impossible to have clear awareness without true obedience... if you are clean inside, what is outside will be cleaned by itself."

Mrs Jansen

The tail-end of autumn.

Many releases.

A surprise.

A new batch of prisoners. A civil engineer, an artistic couple, a couple engaged in the importation of carpets, a former railway station manager.

The charges: the civil engineer - having a Bulgarian mistress.

The artists - being Dutch citizens, of Jewish ancestry.

The carpet importers - having business contacts with Jews based in hostile countries.

A last, faltering attempt on the part of a foolish vassal to curry favour with a defeated overlord.

The station manager - is a renegade Jew.

Mrs Jansen. Painter, mid-thirties. Clear, imperious alto voice. Receives parcels in a steady stream. Dried food, some of which she gives to him. Forbids him, most vehemently, to share it with the engineer, who shares a bunk with him.

The engineer. Has acquaintances in the township nearby. He's invited by the mayor to design a municipal park.

Needs an assistant. Him.

They go down to the township, take measurements.

They're entertained at the mayoral house. A lavish lunch. A rare treasure - a fresh loaf of bread, shared fifty-fifty.

The engineer's paramour turns up at the camp. A bag of nuts, dried fruit, marzipan, biscuits. There's a new sergeant-major. Personal packages are not to be passed.

The paramour goes to bed with the sergeant-major. The package is handed over. The engineer takes out the marzipan. The engineer takes out poppy-cakes. Cuts off a slice for him.

Mrs Jansen.

Pistil - a dried fruit jam roll. A delight to the eye, a treat to the palate. She stuffs it into his hand, says she can't wait to paint his portrait. After liberation, when victory comes.

Pistil. He shares it with the engineer.

Mrs Jansen is angry. Exceedingly angry. Astonished, too. In a loud, clear voice, intended to reach the ears of all present, Mrs Jansen declares, firmly and unequivocally, that the engineer is hoarding his provisions and not sharing them on an equitable basis. After midnight, under cover of darkness, he's gorging himself on marzipan, nuts, biscuits, dried fruits. She's awake. She sees.

The prisoners hear, don't respond.

The engineer hears, doesn't respond.

Mrs Jansen: he should eat the pistil she gives him. By himself. Keep them to himself, the way the engineer does. The pistil - advance payment for a painting she's supposed to be doing. When the time comes. After liberation, after victory.

They are not to be shared.

He pays her no heed.

Jansen the artistic lady. A look in her eyes that is open, steadfast, warm, penetrating, radiating confidence, caressing. Lithe body, round head, average height, sculpted lips.

She longs to paint his portrait, can't wait to paint his portrait, yearns to paint his portrait.

She'll paint him after liberation. When victory comes.

After victory:

His portrait is displayed in an exhibition. Underneath it is the title, "Gavroche". The artist wins a prize for it, awarded by the socialist municipality of Sofia.

The artistic Jansen.

Tries to increase his pistil ration.

He refuses.

She doesn't press him.

The artistic Jansen demands of the camp commandant, a police officer corrupt from head to foot and from foot to head, that space be set aside for a shower.

Her voice is authoritative, imperious, brooking no refusal. Her look direct, sincere, firm, brazen.

The officer sets space aside for a shower. A rectangular structure of planks, crudely nailed together. A hose attached to a pipe, fed by a massive barrel.

Mrs Jansen takes a shower every morning. Soap and cold water. Soap and warm water, from the kitchen.

Sunday morning. After her shower, Mrs Jansen strides up the hill, with purposeful gait. Knocks on the door of the temporary office of the camp commandant, the police officer corrupt from head to foot and from foot to head.

A verbal complaint, a vociferous one. The whole camp hears Mrs Jansen's complaint. The whole camp listens intently to Mrs Jansen's vociferous complaint.

One of the guards has been spying on her, in the shower. She points him out. Demands he be punished!

The camp commandant asks, in a quavering voice, quite unlike his own – what kind of punishment does she have in mind? Mrs Jansen's reply – she's no expert on the punishments meted out to Peeping Toms in the military and the police force. That's his department! Mrs Jansen marches out of his office, giving him no opportunity to respond.

The guard is punished. Severely.

Week-end leave cancelled, an extra week of night sentry-duty. The guard changes his ways, shows himself as meek as a lamb. Whenever he encounters Mrs Jansen, he salutes, a full military style salute, impeccably executed: standing to attention, clicking heels, open palm touching forehead.

Reverence and respect.

Mrs Jansen doesn't respond to his salute. Haughty, untamed, regal.

The Jansens have no children.

They are both painters.

Mr Jansen is the quiet type, has a pipe perpetually clamped between pale lips.

They are content, she with him and he with her.

Mrs Jansen. Her painting of "Gavroche" – awarded a prize by the cultural section of the socialist municipality.

Mrs Jansen and Mr Jansen, deep in debt. Accustomed to debt. Living in a spacious apartment,

in an exclusive district of Sofia. An enthusiast for
their art has put it at their disposal. Rent-free.
They paint. Sink deeper into debt.

A week after the punishment of the peeping guard,
the prisoners are summoned from their bunks.
Midnight parade.
Lines drawn up.
Guards armed with automatic weapons.
Rain lashing bare heads.
Good visibility.
The commandant, the officer corrupt from head
to foot and from foot to head, stands before the lines.
Tries to stand. His body sways from side to side,
back and forth. The officer is as drunk as Lot. In his
shaking hand is a pistol, aimed at the ranks.
Curses and abuse. There will be a reckoning for all
the scoundrels of the world. Jews. Communists. He
won't rest, won't spare any effort. An end to
corruption!
Cold. His bladder is going to burst. The sermon
continues.
Mrs Jansen steps out of the ranks. Confronts the
unsteady pistol of the camp commandant.
You are drunk, Sir! – her voice, a whiplash.
Guards snap to attention. He breaks off in mid-tirade.
You can go back to the shack – the commandant
slurs, his tongue heavy.
Not until you let everyone go!
You can go back...
Mrs Jansen turns to him. The regal severity in her
eyes changes swiftly to a look of infinite affection –
You, you go back to the shack.
He repeats like an echo: Not until everyone is

allowed to go!

The pistol has lost all sense of direction. It's pointing at him now.

Mrs Jansen springs forward like a lioness, standing firm between the waving pistol and the ranks of prisoners.

Dismiss the parade. You're drunk, Sir!

Dismiss!

A wild scramble, as all run in blind confusion, scared and puzzled, prisoners to the shacks, guards to their quarters.

The sergeant-major grips the arm of the commandant who has lost direction, leads him away. They recede.

He hurries to empty his bladder, releases a torrent of urine... sometimes, he can't tell where the piss ends and the rain starts.

Mrs Jansen comes out of the hut. Anxiously. Searching for him.

He call to her: I'm just coming!

She comes closer.

He insists, in a tone leaving no room for objections, that she go back the way she came. She goes back the way she came.

Police officer corrupt from head to foot and from foot to head, after:

Slips through the fingers of the new regime. Disappears. The ground has opened up and swallowed him.

He is hunted, vigorously.

He's arrested on the Turkish border, with five thousand dollars in his possession. Sentenced to a ten year term of imprisonment, including two years of re-education. He emerges from prison a fervent communist. A fascist-hunter.

Does a deal with a clerk at the Canadian Embassy. A thousand dollars for a fake Canadian passport.

The "embassy clerk" is an agent provocateur. The former police officer is sent to a labour camp, suffering acute depression.

Dies a year later.

"Depart from the sensual, abandon the law of the flesh – and the law of freedom will be written in your heart... in a place that is set aside for the spiritual, weakness and despair will find no haven" (Theoleptus of Philadelphia, Fourteenth Century).

Renegade

Short of stature. Steel-framed spectacles. Dismissive look. Not always shaved. Birthplace – Russia. Revolutionary, counter-revolutionary. Past shrouded in mist, very dense mist.

Bulgaria. Attempt to fit in. Jewish communities. Treasurer to the Zionist leadership. Embezzlement of funds. Change of religion: "Dov" becomes "Boris". Active member of anti-Semitic groups. A zealot, sparing no effort to conceal his Jewish origin, to erase it. Denies it vehemently. He calls himself a "railway engineer", claims all kinds of qualifications. Taken on as station manager in an average-size town. Power-struggle with the man originally appointed to the post. He makes it known that the disappointed applicant is a member of a communist cell. Interrogation, trial, prison.

The supporters of the man imprisoned publish a counter-charge: Boris – is a Jew. Interrogation, dismissal. Concentration camp.

He's the talkative kind:

Hitler – is going to settle accounts with the world. Hitler – will not be defeated. Hitler will settle accounts with the Jews. With all the Jews of the world. They're going to be wiped out. Hitler – is on the verge of victory. In his arsenal – a secret, lethal weapon. It's a fact, the Bulgarian government is reconsidering its go-soft policy. The Bulgarian government knows that Hitler's triumph is imminent. A secret weapon, to be unleashed in Communist Russia. A third of Communist Russia will be wiped out. A third will be subjected to lethal contamination. A third - the population will flee in all directions, to all corners of the earth. All the states opposing Hitler will surrender. Capitulate. Fall on their knees and beg for peace. Unconditional peace. Every people, every tongue, nation, country - will serve Hitler. Hitler's slaves. Nazism will rule. Jews from all the nations of the world will be concentrated in the barren third of Communist Russia. Repeated use of the secret weapon. A world cleansed, once and for all, of the Jewish contagion. A world that can breathe easy, freed from the Jewish contagion. Purged of the Jewish contagion.

He knows very well what he's talking about. He knows the Jews inside and out. He was born a Jew.

They don't argue with Boris the renegade. They don't try to contradict the statements of Boris the renegade. Not even with the slightest hint, the lightest of flickers. They listen to the homilies of Boris the renegade. Defiance in their hearts, fear in their hearts, dread in their hearts, hatred in their hearts. Hatred stronger than death.

Guards listen to the words of Boris the renegade. With satisfaction on the outside. In the heart - revulsion and dread. Dread of the unknown. Boris the renegade casts his terror over the entire camp.

Albert the barber. Cuts the hair of everyone who asks for it. Shaves everyone who asks for it. Guards - for free. Prisoners - a tenner.

Renegade Boris has his hair cut. Has a shave.

Refuses to pay.

Albert the barber is angry. He's had enough.

Albert the barber is seething, his wrath overflowing: Hitler is done for! Renegade Boris promises Albert the barber, that when he leaves the camp, he will personally see to it that he is hanged on a tall pillar, on a thick rope, skilfully knotted. He will personally see to it that the surviving prisoners are there to witness the hanging.

Albert the barber refuses to serve Renegade Boris. No more shaves, no more haircuts, even if he pays.

Renegade Boris appeals to the sergeant-major, demands the immediate punishment of Albert the barber. The charge: being a communist agent.

The sergeant-major orders the flogging of Albert the barber. Ten strokes.

Renegade Boris protests. Ten strokes – that's child's play!

The sergeant-major isn't reconsidering.

Ten strokes.

No less, no more.

Albert the barber is flogged in the guards' quarters. Not one of the other prisoners is present. By order.

Renegade Boris protests again. He should be flogged with everyone looking on. Let them see and let them fear.

The sergeant-major isn't reconsidering.

Albert comes out of the guards' quarters hale and hearty. Grinning, from ear to ear. "Ten tickles!" he reports back to his fellow prisoners.

The verdict of Renegade Boris on the sergeant-major: His day will come! The threat reaches the ears of the sergeant-major. No response. Explicit instructions from the high windows. Don't tangle with Boris the renegade.

Renegade Boris plays chess. He's brought a set with him. Takes it out into the yard. A table, two chairs, the board opened out and all the pieces in their places. No one wants to play with him.

He turns to him. Personally.

He takes his seat.

The game begins.

Clarity of thought, such that you wouldn't have thought existed. It would never have occurred to you. You couldn't have imagined it.

Clarity of thought of the camp. Rarefied air, meagre food. Thought unsullied. Thought that is pure, absolute.

The moves of Boris the renegade are marvellously transparent.

Prisoners gather around the players. In stages. Closest are those to whom the game is familiar, who have some expertise at it. Behind them – those who have an idea of what the game is about. Behind them – those who don't know the game at all.

In the first rank – outstanding players of the game, after them – amateurs, after them – the curious.

A dense ring of heads. Tension.

Renegade Boris is in a worsening position. He's lost a bishop and a knight. Defeat is looming, clear as the daylight. The experts know it, so do the amateurs, so do the curious. Quiet, deep satisfaction. A strong sense of schadenfreude.

Before moving his queen, and declaring checkmate, he asks the other, very politely, to put the bishop back in its place, the bishop that has been moved surreptitiously and illegally. Renegade Boris protests vehemently, insisting that he hasn't touched the bishop, and this is an outrageous accusation, unworthy of an intelligent lad. The camp pickpocket testifies quietly, that he saw Boris moving the bishop, under cover of the sleeve of his jacket. He speaks with the measured assurance of one who is well versed in sleight-of-hand techniques – as well as a chess aficionado who knows that according to the rules, the bishop could not possibly be in the square where it is standing,

Waits.

Renegade Boris silently moves the bishop back to its place.

The queen moves without hindrance: Checkmate.

The pickpocket says he would like to play. Boris the renegade makes way for him. Albert the barber organises a tournament. The champion will win a free haircut and shave. The engineer, joining in the tournament, adds to the haircut and shave a poppy-cake and two walnuts.

A list of competitors: Renegade Boris, already knocked out, he, the pickpocket, the engineer, the French teacher with the gammy leg, laconic in-his-forties, Mr Jansen the painter. The game with the pickpocket proceeds smoothly. Thought that is no longer thought. Absolute clarity of consciousness. Definitive. The clarity of consciousness of the camp.

Clarity that isn't human, not of this world, not to be judged by this world's criteria. Not a fair game. Gives an advantage that isn't appropriate, like injecting hormones into athletes at the Olympiad.

He doesn't get up and go. Doesn't concede. Doesn't stop the game.

A swelling crowd of spectators. Descending from their bunks, emerging from their hiding-places, to feast their eyes on the sport.

A social event.

Filling the void. Silly perhaps, even faintly ludicrous, but a social event, something they have all been craving, for as long as they can remember, something which they deserve, from any conceivable perspective, more than any other group of people in the world.

The whole camp is here. There are even a couple of guards, looking on from time to time, wondering perhaps if observing the game is compatible with the rules under which they are supposed to operate, patrolling the camp and keeping a vigilant eye on the prisoners. Their impulse is to watch. Space is made for them, without a word spoken. The guards accept the silent invitation, but are grim-faced, on the lookout for any potential trouble that may arise. When they reach the table where the players are sitting, their stern mood dissolves, all awkwardness is gone. Perhaps they have no idea of what chess is about. Perhaps. But they are breathing the air, taking in the spirit of competition. Tension that tickles the bones, sends a pleasurable thrill through the gut, puts a spark in the eye, stimulates thought, coloured with emotion.

There are no prisoners left in the shack. They're all here. Men and women, old and young. You could hold a census. There isn't room for all of them around the players' table. They're not all watching the game, they're not all familiar with the game. Still, they come down from their bunks and join the crowd.

He has to play. Go on playing. His duty.

He'll have to make his excuses, when the time comes. This clarity isn't natural. It's a fleeting, temporary thing. He knows that for a fact. If only it were an inseparable part of him, of his being, of his consciousness, of his thought, if only!

Checkmate. The pickpocket is beaten.

The pickpocket doesn't believe what he is seeing. Stunned to the marrow of his bones. He says slowly, carefully enunciating every word, every phrase:

You are simply a genius at the game of chess... You should know, till this day I have been beaten by no one... amateur, average, professional. A chess master, undefeated. Until today.

The engineer takes his place.

He is soon beaten. As is the French teacher with the gammy leg, as is laconic in-his-forties, as is the barber.

Mr Jansen sits down facing him.

They make way for Mrs Jansen. She stands beside the players, close at hand.

A look that is open, warm, bold and caressing passes over his face.

Confusion in his heart.

A blessed kind of confusion, inspiring confidence, the desire to excel.

Opening gambits.

Mr Jansen the painter puffs on his pipe. Smoke-rings rise into the air. Mr Jansen is the embodiment of the good and the upright, and the free.

For a moment he considers conceding to him. Feigning defeat. Just for a moment. Mr Jansen's moves are cleverly planned. There will be no need to feign defeat. Mr Jansen is going to win. He's expected to win. Clear prospects for the victory of Mr Jansen. This is becoming an interesting game.

The clarity of the camp doesn't let him down. If only it would!

Interesting game.

Slow.

Very slow, very interesting.

A decisive move escapes the notice of the alert Mr Jansen.

He executes it.

His heart isn't celebrating victory.

Mr Jansen still has a chance.

A slim one.

He has not a shadow of doubt, that if Mr Jansen wins, he will delight in his victory. Not a shadow of a doubt.

Where is Mrs Jansen? Only a moment ago, she was standing between the two of them. She's nowhere to be seen. She's gone. He doesn't want to think about Mrs Jansen. The game goes on.

A delicate, firm hand is laid on his shoulder. A purifying touch. The hand of Mrs Jansen, standing behind him. Engrossed in the game, he didn't notice her moving behind him. And now – her hand on his shoulder. Silky touch.

The game has to be wrapped up, and quickly. If not – his heart will burst, laden as it is with dazzling light, the flood-waters of joy, the brazen spirit of freedom.

Mr Jansen holds out a friendly hand. A pleasant smile on his lips.

Not one of the defeated players has remembered to shake the hand of the victor, except Mr Jansen. Mrs Jansen is blessed with a perfect husband.

Mrs Jansen. Her hand is still on his shoulder.

There and then he has his haircut and shave. Albert the barber makes the comment, that this is the first time, in all his wealth of experience as a barber, he has ever shaved an egg.

The haircut is complete, exposing a high, clean forehead, accentuating the clear lines of the face, an open look capable of penetrating heart and gut.

One of the guards asks to be taught the rules of chess. He promises. When the opportunity arises. Mrs Jansen hands him a packet of pistil. Prize for the victor. Not to be shared with anyone.

Release authorisations are arriving one after another. Renegade Boris is among those to be freed. He's been in the camp just eight days. That's all. Something funny there.

The clothes contributed by the Jewish community of Fleven are distributed according to need. What's left – is raffled. He gets a top hat. He paces too and fro in a silk shirt, white long-johns and top hat, to the accompaniment of gales of laughter.

Renegade Boris wants the hat. Offers in exchange a striped, red handkerchief.

Nothing doing.

He leaves the hat on the bunk.

Goes out for a while.

Comes back. No hat.

He confers with the pickpocket.

The pickpocket will have no difficulty opening the suitcase of Renegade Boris. All he needs is a safety-pin.

He has a safety-pin.

Renegade Boris is called to the sergeant-major's office, to receive his release papers, sign for them.

He and the pickpocket crouch over the suitcase of Renegade Boris.

Carefully the pickpocket inserts the curved end of

an open safety-pin into the left-hand lock, then the right.

The suitcase springs open. There is the hat, crushed beneath Boris's overcoat.

The pickpocket turns his attention to the coat. A razor in his hand. He runs the blade along the back-stitching that holds the two halves of the coat together, from top to bottom.

The coat is put back in its place.

He has retrieved the hat.

They lock the case, leave it in its place, go away.

Renegade Boris.

A look of smug satisfaction.

He has the release-papers in his hand, Hitler has not been defeated, there will yet be an end to the Jews. A world purged of Jews. What a relief that will be! Last words.

A bright morning. Renegade Boris rises early. He has to prepare himself for the journey. Get down to the town on time. Wait for the train.

The suitcase is opened. A puzzled, anxious glance. Prying eyes. All the occupants of the shack are watching him, tense, motionless. They all know. It was all done before their eyes.

Renegade Boris takes out the coat. His mind distracted, he puts it on, locks the case, sets out on its way.

A loud peal of laughter accompanies his steps. A laugh than which nothing could be more pure, more captivating, more genuine. A laugh of joyful, decisive victory over a thoroughly detestable foe.

The thick overcoat, woven from the finest fabric, is wide open, all down the back.

Renegade Boris turns, discovers the two flapping

wings of his overcoat.

A tirade of blazing hatred. You're all going to end up on the scaffold. You're all going to die, in agony. I promise you that!

The two halves of the coat are joined with safety-pins. Renegade Boris leaves the shack. Fresh air, fit to breathe.

"The ultimate separation is separation from separation. Man will see in it neither loss nor gain. But whosoever leaves behind the vanities of this world and thinks that he has left something, is exaggerating the importance of this world, which in the view of the prophets, is nothing at all" (al-Ghazali, 1058-1111).

Renegade Boris, After

Drawing on his record as a concentration camp inmate, he has no difficulty finding employment in the transport department. As a fervent communist, and a talented Nazi-basher, he rises rapidly in the ranks of the Party.

His reputation reaches the ears of Albert the barber. He contacts the authorities, testifies.

Boris the renegade is arrested. The former camp sergeant-major, sentenced to twenty years imprisonment with hard labour, is summoned to give evidence. He is brought in chains from his cell to the interrogator's office, testifies. Boris the renegade is unperturbed. He reveals to the interrogator his closely guarded secret. Boris the renegade was an agent of the "Cheka", smuggled into Bulgaria with the purpose of infiltrating the apparatus of the Fascist regime. His mission necessarily involved a great deal of pretence, and he played the role of the Nazi extremist to perfection. He advanced to the very heart of Fascist intelligence, reaching the higher echelons of the Bulgarian counter-espionage service.

Renegade Boris produces a document dating back to the twenties, bearing the seal of the Russian Cheka.

The interrogator is confused. He refers the file to his superiors, they refer it to the minister. The minister refers it to the government of the Soviet Union.

The reply is slow in coming. Renegade Boris is held under house-arrest. A month. Two months. At the beginning of the third month, he is visited by two young men in their thirties. Smart grey suits, athletic build, tight lips, blank expression. They lift him up bodily with arms thick as an elephant's leg, push him into a giant Zil, the last word in Soviet transport. An authentic replica of the Mercedes. They drive to a military airfield. Fly to Moscow.

Renegade Boris disappears.

Renegade Boris - the end.

"He who denies himself utterly, gains at once all that is good and pleasing to God, even before he begins the life of spiritual struggle. Obedience means not believing that any good thing can come about from your own efforts, however long you may live" (Brother Kallistos and Brother Agnastos, monks of the Fourteenth Century).

Liberation

Autumn drawing to an end. Winter approaching. The air clears. Rain falls quietly, equably. Heat recedes, goes on receding. Mordant cold, not unpleasant. Impossible to leave the shack without outer clothing. They go out anyway.

Releases. New list.

The Jansens, the French teacher with the gammy leg, the carpet importer, some new faces, recent arrivals and – him!

In the evening, those due for release are summoned to sign for receipt of their certificates. Pick up free travel tickets.

A guard reads the list of all those who are to report to the camp commandant's office.

All the names.

Except his.

The camp-commandant isn't calling him, although his name is on the list. His name, it turns out, has been misspelt. A letter omitted. The last letter of his father's name. The commandant doesn't want to risk anything. The release order will be returned to his superiors with a question mark in place of the missing letter. Superiors will refer it to their superiors, who will send it back to the central office, to be buried at the bottom of a file.

He has no hope of ever getting out of here.

He'll be forgotten.

His existence will be forgotten.

His face falls.

Mrs Jansen. Looks devastated. Intense suffering. His own look – utter despair.

Tries to approach him. He rebuffs her brusquely.

Asks a simple question. Voice hollow, depressed. Embittered by his despair.

His lips are sealed.

The pickpocket intervenes. Explains to Mrs Jansen what's going on.

She goes storming up to the top of the hill.

Mrs Jansen. Bursts into the camp commandant's office. Walks to the other side of the desk. The camp-commandant is stunned into silence, frozen, refusing to believe what he's seeing. The list of releases in front of him.

In front of her, now.

She locates his name, takes a pen, deftly adds the missing letter.

That's it, Sir! – she declares – He'll be reporting along with the rest of them! He's to be released along with the rest of them!

He reports along with the rest of them.

Gets a release certificate, as they all do. Gets a free voucher for rail travel, as they all do. Released, as they all are.

Leaves the commandant's office. Outside.

Soft air, purple twilight. Tomorrow, at this time, he'll be on his way to freedom, saying goodbye to his fellow inmates, to the camp, to this unique phase of his life. Life of a sub-animal, in the company of sub-animals.

Standing still on the hill-top.

Quiet breeze. Submissive, caressing.

His wits haven't returned to him yet.

Mrs Jansen approaches.

Stands behind him. Very close.

With a delicate movement, so firm as to be both irresistible and ineluctable, she turns him to face her.

Face to face.

Eye to eye

Look to look.

Unflagging joy. Eternity.

Arms of the world, rising slowly and surely.

No barriers.

Embrace. Bold, intense, complete.

Sapphire horizons, splitting apart.

Height.

Fragrance of flowers that don't yet have a name.

Nothing is missing from her embrace. Tangible or intangible, truthful and holding no vestige of the truth. Fleeting. Everlasting.

The kind of embrace that is earned once in the course of an exceptional life, or not earned at all.

A fervent kiss on virginal lips. Destroying all, restoring all. Never to be erased.

On top of the hill. Before the eyes of the police officer, commandant of the camp. Before the eyes of the guards, staring and bemused. Before the eyes of the prisoners, who have just received their certificates of release and free rail-tickets, as he has. Before the eyes of the rest of the prisoners, who have come out from their dismal shacks to watch them, the pair of them. To soar with them. To be them. If only it were possible.

Top of the hill.

Fresh grass.

Free breeze.

Violet evening.

Fragrance of stars.

A sincere, brave, proud, all-conquering embrace. In full view of all. Realisation of a vision craved since time immemorial. On the demise of an old world, whose master is death, comes the turn of truth and love, a world over which death has no dominion, where justice resides.

Bright morning.

He has no baggage.

Saying their farewells to everyone. Taking their leave of everyone. One after the other. Handshakes – firm, flaccid, damp, dry. Contorted faces. Weeping.

The pickpocket comes out to accompany him part of the way. As far as he is allowed. The fence.

Encouraging one another.

Declaring with confidence that his release too is not far away.

Replying with confidence that he hasn't the slightest doubt he'll be released soon, the time will come.

Mind you don't make any mistakes at the last moment!

He won't make mistakes. Not any more. Especially – not at the last moment.

Hearts awkward, still in shock.

And you – have a life! A slap on the shoulder. Eyes moist.

All of a sudden – a hug. Firm, manly, reassuring.

Separating from one another.

And you – watch out for pickpockets!

The pickpocket weeps.

He weeps.

Shacks.
Beyond the fence – they are dwarfed.
Contemptible. The whiteness of abandoned bones.
Rain. Quiet. Light, serene, purifying.
Rain.
Lifting his head high. Soft grey clouds scudding over the broad expanse. Drops sliding over exposed face, trickling between lips, willingly opened. Swallowing hope, space, freshness, strength.
Mist. Descending on the hill, thickening, sliding over it, engulfing it completely.
Must make a move.
A free man.

"God –
make me a channel of thy peace
that where there is hatred, I may bring love
that where there is wrong, I may bring the spirit of forgiveness
that where there is discord, I may bring harmony
that where there is error, I may bring truth
that where there is doubt, I may bring faith
that where there is despair, I may bring hope
that where there are shadows, I may bring light
that where there is sadness, I may bring joy.
God –
grant that I may seek rather to comfort than to be comforted
to understand, than to be understood

to love, than to be loved
For it is by self-forgetting that one finds
It is by forgiving that one is forgiven
It is by dying that one awakens to Eternal Life.
God -
Grant me the Serenity to accept the things I cannot
change
Courage to change the things I can
And wisdom to know the difference.
Grant me the joy of happiness.
To love and to revere You.
All my days and my nights.
(Francis of Assisi, 1181/2-1226)

Athar

Eighteen... nineteen... twenty... twenty-one...
Seventy-three to eighty-two. The contents of a bunch
of grapes. No more, no less. Half a kilo. A bunch. Just
the one. Seventy-three to eighty-two units
A distant sorrow.
Twenty-two... twenty-three... twenty-four...
No escape. The tangible always comes to an end.
It has a beginning, it has an ending. It emerges into
the light of the world, grows, burgeons, prospers,
withers, crumbles, fades, disappears. What is not
perceived by the senses – has no beginning, no ending.
It does not grow, does not burgeon, does not prosper,
does not wither, does not crumble, does not fade, does
not disappear.
Ephemeral.
Eternal.
A young twilight.
Violet.
Early autumn.
Twenty-five... twenty-six... twenty-seven... twenty-
eight... in less than an hour from now – parade.
Distribution of bread. In less than half an hour from
now – the gate will open and a cart hitched to a horse
will roll into the compound of the camp. Food
supplies for the guards.
Twenty-nine... thirty... thirty-one... thirty-two...
thirty-three...
At the narrow bend, by the ruined walls of his den,

he will lie in wait for the cart. Perform a brisk, accurate, agile, virtuoso leap. Concealed from the sight of the carter. No one could match his expertise at leaping on a moving cart. At the age of six he was hitching rides on wagons speeding down the street, demonstrating his superiority over the neighbourhood children watching him. What fun, what a lark! Hoodwinking the carter, getting away before his whip catches up with him.

Everything learned in life, is an asset.

Jumping on a cart.

Time brings changes to fruition.

No repression, no survival.

No time. For surrender, no time. For defeat, no time. For victory, no time.

Thirty-four... thirty-five... thirty-six... forty... fifty... sixty... seventy... eighty... eighty-one...

Naked stalk. Empty thorns.

Hunger.

Concentration camp.

Hunger.

The cart bringing supplies for the guards is due to arrive at any moment.

He abandons his hiding-place.

Crouches in the shadow of the narrow bend.

Creak of an iron gate.

The cart is inside, moving towards him.

Don't attract the attention of the carter. A tomato or two, from the tomato box. A cucumber or two, from the cucumber box. An onion is unfit. A potato, likewise. You can't eat a live potato on an empty stomach, or on a full or a half-full stomach. He's tried. He spewed up his guts. The camp pickpocket promises he'll devise a way of softening a live potato. A method.

An abstract promise. Not fulfilled. Not yet fulfilled. The camp pickpocket. Seventeen years old. Fingers of a virtuoso pianist, rubber body of a circus acrobat, brain of Einstein. One day, he'll discover a way of softening a live potato, making it edible. Then he'll filch a few of them from the open potato-sack. One, two, three, four. Not more than four. Time doesn't permit. The guards are liable to notice.

Time brings changes to fruition. The acute intelligence of the camp pickpocket will bring a plan to fruition. Fingers of a virtuoso pianist, body of a circus acrobat, brain of Einstein.

The cart bringing the guards' provisions...

An accurate leap. Soft landing, like a cat.

The carter takes no notice.

Consciously or unconsciously.

Guards take no notice of an absent cucumber, a missing tomato.

The carter – a noble creature.

One tomato and another. In the pocket. One cucumber and another, in the other pocket. Don't touch the meat! Take care. Guards don't tolerate changes to their routine! Guards won't go without their meat ration! Not such much as a milligram. Have some self-control. Don't touch the meat.

Raw meat. He could gorge himself on it, without a second thought. Same with the bread. Don't touch those loaves – they've been counted! Don't be tempted!

The carter isn't giving the game away. In a world of betrayal and shattered limbs, he's no quisling. He notices the hunched shadow, poised to jump, turns the horse in the most convenient direction, slows the pace. He won't give the game away.

The carter. Not confined to the camp. Unlike him and his partners in destiny.

If he were to be imprisoned, he'd be changed beyond recognition, like him and his partners in destiny. No longer a noble creature. Or perhaps – he wouldn't change, would he?

Time to leave.

Jump out.

Two cucumbers, two tomatoes.

The carter lashes his horse, picks up speed again.

Everything has gone smoothly.

For how long?

You don't ask questions in the camp.

You don't ask "How long?"

"How long?" doesn't exist.

"Tomorrow will take care of itself," the Scriptures tell us. A sublime principle, a commandment, a rule. One that's upheld in the camp, in the spirit and in the letter, in theory and in practice. Not as in the world outside the camp. As distinct from the world outside the camp. In contrast to the world outside the camp.

Only in the camp is it upheld automatically, without sermons and homilies, necessarily, inevitably, naturally. Without coercion, pretence, self-abasement. Upheld by free will, pure and absolute.

The camp – a sacred site.

Athar.

The only one in the whole world.

The one and the only.

Athar.

SHLOMO KALO

God is love and he who dwells in love dwells in God
and God in him
(First Epistle of John, IV, 16).

About the Author

Shlomo Kalo (1928-2014) was born in Sofia, Bulgaria. From the age of 12, was active in an anti-Fascist underground. At the age of 15, was arrested and exiled to a concentration camp. At the age of 18, won a prize in a poetry competition. Studied medicine in Prague where he also worked as a journalist. As an overseas volunteer for the newly established Israel he was sent to train as a pilot in Olomouc. Kalo immigrated to Israel in 1949. He was awarded M.Sc. in microbiology by the Tel-Aviv University and later became director of medical laboratories in Israel's largest health care service.

The sharp turn in his life which occurred in the first week of 1969 has been reflected ever since in his creation. 80 books of his were published in Israel: Literary fiction and literary non-fiction on a variety of themes, novels, literature for younger readers, philosophy, translations, "The Documented Story". Rights of his titles were purchased in 16 countries.

During the last years of his life Shlomo Kalo was nominated for the Nobel Prize in Literature.

www.ingramcontent.com/pod-product-compliance
Lightning Source LLC
LaVergne TN
LVHW051235080426
835513LV00016B/1594